THE UNCOMMON WISDOM OF
RONALD REAGAN

Edited by Bill Adler

THE KENNEDY WIT

THE UNCOMMON WISDOM OF JACQUELINE KENNEDY ONASSIS

THE UNCOMMON WISDOM OF
RONALD REAGAN

A Portrait in His Own Words

BILL ADLER, EDITOR

LITTLE, BROWN AND COMPANY
Boston   New York   Toronto   London

First Edition

Excerpts from *Grinning with the Gipper* by James S. Denton and Peter Schweizer:
Copyright © 1988 by James S. Denton and Peter Schweizer.
Reprinted by permission of Grove/Atlantic, Inc.

Excerpts from *An American Life*, *Speaking My Mind*, and *Where's the Rest of Me?*
are reprinted by permission of Nancy and Ronald Reagan.

Library of Congress Cataloging-in-Publication Data

Reagan, Ronald.
    The uncommon wisdom of Ronald Reagan: a portrait in his own words/
Bill Adler, editor. — 1st ed.
        p.   cm.
    ISBN 0-316-05600-6
    1. Reagan, Ronald — Quotations.   2. Presidents—United States —
Quotations.   I. Adler, Bill.   II. Title.
E838.5.R432   1996
973.927'092 — dc20   96-575

10   9   8   7   6   5   4   3   2   1

BP
*Published simultaneously in Canada
by Little, Brown & Company (Canada) Limited*

Printed in the United States of America

CONTENTS

Contents

INTRODUCTION

Ronald Wilson Reagan once said: "I wasn't a great communicator, but I communicated great things, and they didn't spring full-blown from my brow, they came from the heart of a great nation — from our experience, our wisdom, and our belief in the principles that have guided us for two centuries. They called it the Reagan Revolution. Well, I'll accept that, but for me it always seemed more like the great rediscovery, a rediscovery of our values and our common sense."

The wisdom Reagan brought to "the Revolution" did not spring up suddenly as a strategy for a political campaign. It was based on the experiences of his lifetime. Who better to tell us of those experiences than the great communicator himself, who always had time to spin a good yarn.

So, without further ado, Ronald Reagan will tell you his tale himself.

THE UNCOMMON WISDOM OF
RONALD REAGAN

THE EARLY YEARS

As a boy and as a young man, Ronald Wilson Reagan had a playful spirit, a sense of adventure, and was a keen observer. All of these characteristics would help him to develop his wit and talent for telling stories, which began to emerge once he reached Eureka College. His sense of humor and the faith his parents instilled in him helped him in his youth, after college, and when he got to the competitive world of Hollywood.

Childhood

Ronald Wilson Reagan was born February 6, 1911, in Tampico, Illinois. His family moved around quite a bit, but when he was nine, the family moved to Dixon, Illinois, which Reagan came to consider his hometown.

"To me it was heaven. . . . It was a small universe where I learned standards and values that would guide me for the rest of my life."

∾

Reagan was born in a flat above the local bank in Tampico, Illinois:

"According to family legend, when my father ran up the stairs and looked at his newborn son, he quipped: 'He looks like a fat little Dutchman. But who knows, he might grow up to be President someday.'"

∾

As a child, Reagan asked people to call him "Dutch":

"I never thought 'Ronald' was rugged enough for a young red-blooded American boy."

∽

The Reagans moved quite a bit during Ronald's childhood:

"My father was constantly searching for a better life, and I was forever the new kid in school. We moved to wherever my father's ambition took him."

∽

The family moved to Chicago when Reagan was two. There he was exposed to the exciting and congested urban world:

"Once, while watching a clanging horse-drawn fire engine race past me with a cloud of steam rising behind it, I decided that it was my intention in life to become a fireman."

∽

One of Reagan's fondest memories as a child was playing mock combat with toy soldiers:

"To this day I get a little thrill out of seeing a cabinet full of toy soldiers."

∽

Reagan's love for toy soldiers may have something to do with the fact that he was growing up during World War I:

"Like almost every other American during those years, I was filled with pride every time I heard a band play 'Over There' or I thought of our doughboys crossing the Atlantic on a noble mission to save our friends in Europe."

～

"Once my mother picked me up and gave me a penny, which I gave to a soldier, saying in my small voice, 'Good luck.'"

～

"I think the realization that some of those boys to whom I waved on the troop train later died on European soil made me an isolationist for a long time."

～

In his autobiography *An American Life* Reagan recalls an experience he had soon after the family left Chicago and moved to the country which gave him an appreciation for the natural world that would stay with him for the rest of his life:

"In the attic of the house, a previous tenant — an anonymous benefactor to whom I owe much — had left behind a huge collection of birds' eggs and butterflies enclosed in glass cases. Mentally appropriating the collections, I escaped for hours at a time into the attic, marveling at the rich colors of the eggs and the intricate and fragile wings of the butterflies. The experience left me with a reverence for the handiwork of God that never left me."

～

"As I look back on those days in Dixon, I think my life was as sweet and idyllic as it could be, as close as I could imagine for a young boy to the world created by Mark Twain in *The Adventures of Tom Sawyer.*"

While Reagan compared the world he grew up in to that in *The Adventures of Tom Sawyer,* it could be said that in his youth, Reagan showed some of Tom's mischievous spirit:

One Fourth of July, Reagan was lighting some prohibited fireworks when a car pulled up and the driver ordered him to get in: "I'd been taught not to get into automobiles with strangers, and refused. When he flashed a police badge, I got in the car."

Reagan was not yet the master of diplomacy he grew up to be. "As we started to drive away, I said, 'Twinkle, twinkle, little star, who in the hell do you think you are.'"

～

Reagan, speaking to the building trades, talked about his first summer job:

"I was fourteen years old, working for an outfit remodeling homes for sale. Before the summer ended, I'd laid hardwood floors, shingled roofs, painted ceilings, and dug foundations.

"There wasn't a very clear distinction in those days between craft lines in a small town. There also weren't any bulldozers or skip loaders in those days, so the grading was pretty much pick and shovel.

"I remember one hot morning I'd been swinging a pick for about four hours. I heard the noon whistle blow. I had been waiting for that sound. I had the pick over my shoulder ready for the next blow, and when I heard the whistle, I just let go, walked out from underneath it, and let it fall behind me.

"I heard a loud scream and then some very profane language. I turned around, and the boss was standing right behind me. That pick was embedded in the ground right between his feet. Two inches either way and I'd have nailed him.

"I remembered the incident when I heard the screams about our budget cuts."

~

"I have a warm spot for school principals. I was in the principal's office once in Dixon High School, and I wasn't there just to pass the time of day. Well, at one point he said to me, 'You know, I don't care what you think of me now, I'm only interested in what you think of me fifteen years from now.'"

~

To participants in the National YMCA Youth Governor's Conference on June 21, 1984:

"I was the drum major, and my brother — he played the bass horn. And I had an incident when we were in a neighboring town on Decoration Day — we were leading the parade. And the marshal of the parade, on his horse, had ridden back to see how everything was coming. And he didn't get back to see how everything was coming. And he didn't get back quite up to the head of the parade in time. And there I was, waving the baton. I knew that the music was sounding further and further away. He had come in time to turn the band but not me. And I was walking down the street all by myself, and the band had turned the corner."

~

In his autobiography *Where's the Rest of Me?*, Reagan reflected on his passion for football:

"I never thought seriously about retiring from the junior mayhem, but I managed to time my charge so that I was in one of the upper layers of bodies. The lure of sweat and action always pulled me back to the game — despite the fact that I was a scrawny, undersized, underweight nuisance. As a result, I had a collection of the largest purplish-black bruises possible. More than once, I must have been a walking coagulation. Those were the happiest days of my life."

~

In an interview in 1984 Reagan recalled getting his first gun:

"It was the prize for a Labor Day swimming race near Dixon, Illinois, when I was in high school. I retired as a lifeguard that afternoon just so I could enter the race, and I won that rifle.

"[I used it for] plinking. But on one occasion another fellow and I decided, and this was winter and the river hadn't frozen yet, that we were going to try our hand at self-sustaining camping. We canoed up the river, and that day it turned freezing cold. There was a point we picked out where we would try to get some squirrels, which would be our dinner that night. We did get some squirrels, and I got my first squirrel with my rifle, but by the time we were ready to eat that night, the squirrels were frozen stiff. Then my more experienced companion went down in his duffel bag and came out with a quart fruit jar filled with stew, which his mother had given him. We warmed it and were grateful for it, and the next day we had to cancel our trip and start downriver, because we had to break ice to get the canoe back out in the river. That was about my only real hunting with that gun, but just having it was enough."

~

Reagan recalled his "worst experience as a boy":

"It was the day my father bought a carload of secondhand potatoes for a personal speculation. My brother and I were ordered to the siding to sort the good potatoes from the bad. It was a unique experience. No one who has not sat in a stinking boxcar during hot summer days, gingerly gripping tubers that dissolve in the fingers with a dripping squish, emitting an odor worse than that of a decaying corpse, can possibly imagine the agony we suffered. We did this hideous chore for days. At last we got so queasy at the look of spuds that we simply lied about the rest and dumped them all, good or bad. My father made a little money on the proposition. We got a near-permanent dislike for potatoes in any form. Anyone having trouble staying on a diet should take one whiff of a spoiled potato."

~

Reagan was "a sucker for hero worship." He admired many great historical figures and constantly read about them:

"All in all, as I look back, I realize that my reading left an abiding belief in the triumph of good over evil. There were heroes who lived by standards of morality and fair play."

~

The Early Years

From Reagan's autobiography *An American Life:*

"I grew up observing how the love and common sense of purpose that unites families is one of the most powerful glues on earth and that it can help them overcome the greatest of adversities."

Family

The Reagan family consisted of Reagan's parents, Jack and Nelle, Ronald, and his older brother, Neil. They were a close family, held together by love and the values instilled by Jack and Nelle.

"Ours was a free family that loved each other up to the point where the independence of each member began. For as long as I can remember, [my parents and I] were on a first-name basis with each other."

∾

Reagan said that his parents constantly drummed into him the importance of judging people as individuals:

"There was no more grievous sin at our household than a racial slur or other evidence of religious or racial intolerance. My mother and my father urged my brother and me to bring home our black playmates, to consider them equals, and to respect the religious views of our friends, whatever they were. A lot of it, I think, was because my dad had learned what discrimination was like firsthand. He'd grown up in an era when some stores still had signs at their door saying, NO DOGS OR IRISHMEN ALLOWED."

∾

The Early Years

In his autobiography *An American Life* Reagan writes of his father:

"I learned from my father the value of hard work and ambition, and maybe a little something about telling a story."

∾

"From my mother, I learned the value of prayer, how to have dreams and believe I could make them come true."

∾

In reference to his parents' having never graduated from school:

"No diploma was needed for kindness, in [my mother's] opinion, just as my father believed energy and hard work were the only ingredients needed for success."

∾

Reagan said his mother always looked for and found the goodness in people:

"She always expected to find the best in people and often did, even among the prisoners at our local jail, to whom she frequently brought hot meals."

∾

"While my father was filled with dreams of making something of himself, [my mother] had a drive to help my brother and me make something of ourselves."

∾

Reagan refers to his father as having a lot of "street smarts":

"He was restless, always ready to pull up stakes and move on in search of a better life for himself and his family."

∽

Reagan's father was not fond of politicians:

"My dad believed passionately in the rights of the individual and the working man, and he was suspicious of established authority, especially the Republican politicians who ran the Illinois state government, which he considered as corrupt as Tammany Hall."

∽

At a White House meeting with women leaders of Christian religious organizations on October 13, 1983, Reagan said:

"Nelle Reagan, my mother, God rest her soul, had an unshakable faith in God's goodness. And while I may have not realized it in my youth, I know now that she planted that faith very deeply in me. She made the most difficult Christian message seem very easy."

∽

Reagan recalled the first time his father discovered his son could read:

"I remember my father coming into the house one day before I entered school and finding me on the living room floor with a newspaper in front of me. 'What are you doing?' he asked, and I said, 'Reading the paper.' Well, I imagine he thought I was being a bit of a smart aleck, so he said, 'Okay, read something to me,' and I did. The next thing I knew, he was flying out the front door and from the porch inviting all our neighbors to come over and hear his five-year-old son read."

～

Reagan quite possibly inherited his love of performing from his mother:

"She was the star performer of a group in Dixon that staged what we called 'readings': Dixonites would memorize dramatic or humorous passages from famous poems, plays, speeches, or books and deliver them in a dramatic fashion before an audience at church or elsewhere.

"Whether it was low comedy or high drama, Nelle really threw herself into a part. She loved it. Performing, I think, was her first love."

Nelle Reagan had to keep a close eye on her adventure-loving sons:

"The fascination of the railroad tracks and station [that lay just beyond the park across from their house] was too much to resist. In a toddling expedition, my brother and I crawled under a train snorting steam in the station. We got to the other side just before it gave a mighty jerk and chuffed out. Our narrow escape would have been all right except that Nelle saw us. She nearly collapsed in the kitchen. She caught up with us as we were swiping bits of ice from the ice wagon (our target for the day) and ear-lifted us home."

～

Reagan's father was a shoe salesman:

"And you know, people think, a shoe salesman, but he'd talk to people and they'd come to him and say, 'I'm having this pain here and this problem right over there,' and he would diagnose it and get them the right shoes, and their aches would go away."

~

In Reagan's *Where's the Rest of Me?*, he says of his father:

"He believed literally that all men were created equal and that the man's own ambition determined what happened to him after that. He put his principles into practice."

~

Reagan recalled a time when his father was trying to make money on the road as a shoe salesman:

"He checked into a small-town hotel. 'Fine,' said the clerk, reversing the register and reading his name. 'You'll like it here, Mr. Reagan. We don't permit a Jew in the place.' My father picked up his suitcase again. 'I'm a Catholic,' he said furiously, 'and if it's come to the point where you won't take Jews, you won't take me, either.' Since it was the only hotel in town, he spent the night in his car in the snow. He contracted near-pneumonia and a short time later had the first heart attack of the several that led to his death."

~

Nelle and Jack instilled in their sons the idea that all people are created equal:

"At our one local movie theater, blacks and whites had to sit apart — the blacks in the balcony. My brother's best friend was black, and when they went to the movies, Neil sat with him in the balcony."

∾

When Reagan was in high school, the family moved to the north side of Dixon. Reagan was assigned to the Northside school campus, but to his relief, his older brother decided to remain at the Southside campus:

"Although he and I were close, he was still my older — and bigger — brother, and we had our share of brotherly fistfights and rivalries. He had always had an outspoken, self-confident personality that was a little like Jack's [his father], which made him a natural leader, and until then, I think I probably felt a little under his shadow. On my own at Northside, I knew I wouldn't have to be compared with him."

∾

In an interview many years later, when Reagan himself was a father and grandfather, the reporter asked him about what parents today need to do for their children. Reagan's response reveals what he learned from his parents' example:

"Parents today do best what parents have always done best — that is to love, to provide, to guide, and to take pride in their children. Of course this is done in a multitude of ways — from reading bedtime stories and sharing in sports, to eating together and learning table manners. These familiar family practices create a bond between parent and child that establishes in the child a secure sense of well being."

College

Reagan arrived at Eureka College in the fall of 1928 and was given a needy-student scholarship that covered half of his expenses. He was once accused of majoring in extracurricular activities, but he actually majored in economics and graduated in 1932.

~

On May 8, 1982, Reagan went back to Eureka College to speak at an alumni dinner. His reflections on the event:

"This was pure heaven for me. I genuinely enjoy reminiscing and I did my share of it that evening. I love Eureka College. It's a very small school without a national Ivy League reputation, but if I had to do it all over again, I'd go right back there for my education. The advantage of a smaller school is that you can't be anonymous. Everybody is a part of college life."

At a scholarship fund-raising dinner at Eureka College on September 9, 1986:

"But one thing I'll always cherish about Eureka College besides lessons in football and humility is that the college took a chance on me. Now, my family couldn't pay for the schooling. We didn't live on the wrong side of the tracks, but we lived close enough that we could hear the whistles."

~

"I ended up participating as a freshman in the first student protest in the history of my college.

"But before you decide you're face-to-face with a student radical, let me say that even now, in hindsight, I believe our cause was just. And we didn't break a single window, and we had no picket lines, and we didn't carry any placards or signs."

∾

During his remarks at a White House reception opening the "Champions of American Sport" exhibition on June 22, 1981, Reagan said:

"We didn't have athletic scholarships in those days. We had to do things like wind the clock in the gym."

∾

Winding the clock wasn't the only job Reagan had when he was in school. In his remarks and a question-and-answer session with members of the Massachusetts High Technology Council in Bedford on January 26, 1983, Reagan said:

"I look back and I feel sorry for some of the young people today, because one of the better jobs I ever had in my life was the job I had working my way through college. I washed dishes in the girls' dormitory."

∾

During his remarks at the White House reception opening the "Champions of American Sport" exhibition on June 22, 1981, Reagan said:

"I couldn't play baseball because I couldn't see well enough. That's why I turned to football. The ball was bigger, and so were the fellows."

∾

Reagan was chatting with the National Council of Negro Women when he recalled an old friend with whom he had played football in college — his name was Franklin Burghardt:

"In those days not very many of us got to college, and if you did, it was because you could play football or something, which was how I got there.

"Anyway, Burky was black, and he meant a lot to us, his teammates. We were playing a game one day, down 14 to 0, with only two minutes remaining in the half.

"The other team, which wasn't blessed with someone like Burky, began to pick on him, which was common for the time.

"To give you an indication of what we all thought of Burky, we ended the half 14 to 14 and ended the game 43 to 14 — he was quite a man."

$\sim$

"There was a big gala watermelon hunt. We herded a few carefully indoctrinated freshmen out into the country by night and indicated a plot where we could swipe some of the bulging fruit from the vine. We tiptoed through the patch to build up suspense, and at a prearranged location the place exploded with light. A shotgun blast went off. An upperclassman near me collapsed with a scream, gripping his chest, red fluid flowing slowly between his fingers. 'I'm shot,' he screamed. 'My God, I am shot!' To add to his overacting, a flashlight gave a quick look at his catsup-covered midsection. A well-trained supporting cast, using some version of subliminal selling, shoved the freshmen towards the road, screaming, 'Get help — a doctor — run back to town!' Other things were said, but these were the key words, repeated often enough to stick.

"The frosh took off like leaves before the wind, propelled by fear and charity. We ran a few steps, then let them get ahead and watched them disappear. We hiked back to town by another and shorter road.

"This particular night the freshmen ran nearly eight miles, probably setting some unofficial record (we never bothered to time them). But one fellow had retained his wits long enough to duck into a farmhouse on the main road halfway back to the college. He had wakened the old boy and they phoned the doctor in town, giving the location of the shooting and all the lurid details. Through the night, on his errand of mercy, sped the doctor. The slower return trip gave him time to do a little two-plus-two-comes-up-college type of figuring. At the end of that month, each fraternity on the campus received a bill. It read: 'For battle, murder, and sudden death at the watermelon patch — $10.' Each fraternity paid without protest."

~

"Back at Eureka College when I was playing football one night, we were having a chalk talk with our coach:

"I had never gone into a game in my life that I hadn't said a prayer, but I wouldn't have said so to the guys around me. I thought I was probably the only one in the world who ever did that. Somehow the subject came up about prayer. I sat there and listened. Every fellow in that room, it developed, did the same thing.

"Now, I know what I'd figured out for myself should be a prayer. You can't ask to win because the Lord's got to be on everyone's side, but there are things you can ask. And one by one, every one of us, on our own and never having admitted it before, had come up with the same idea.

"You can't ask to win, but you can ask that He help you to do your best and, having done your best, you'll have no regrets no matter how it turns out, and you will be content with the outcome. Just may it be the best one."

After College

Reagan graduated from college in the thick of the depression, when jobs were hard to find and spirits around the country were low. Although he wasn't sure what he wanted to do at first, his perseverance eventually landed him a job that set him on the path to Hollywood and all that followed.

One summer, a friend's husband, Sid, from Dixon, got Reagan thinking about the future:

"Sid brought my future into the conversation one golden summer evening, sitting on the edge of the pier. He uttered what were not only hopeful words for me, but what was literally the first note of optimism I'd heard about the state of the Union. He said, 'This depression isn't going to last forever, and smart businessmen are willing to take on young men who can learn their business in order to have trained manpower on hand when things start to roll.' After a pause he asked, 'What do you think you'd like to do?' There it was — the question for which I had no answer. All I could do was say, 'I don't know.'"

∾

After Reagan graduated from college, he left his home in Dixon for his first job hunt. He had decided on one field:

"I hitchhiked to Chicago after the swimming season ended with visions of getting a job as a radio announcer. But all I got was rejection: no one wanted an inexperienced kid, especially during the depression. And so I hitchhiked back to Dixon in a storm, my dreams all but smothered by this introduction to reality."

~

Serendipity plays a large role in everyone's life, former Presidents included. Montgomery Ward had just turned him down for a job in Dixon. Reagan then left Dixon and finally found a job — as a radio announcer: "I was about as low as I could be," Reagan said. "Many times, I thought, had I got the job in the Montgomery Ward store, I probably still would be working there."

Reagan had a lot to learn about truth in broadcasting:

"I remember my first experience with broadcasting the truth as a sports announcer. Using the telegraph, I submit that I told the truth — it was just attractively packaged.

"In those days of radio you had a sound-effects man in the studio. He had a wheeled cart, and on it he had every kind of device in the world for the studio dramas, from coconut shells that he beat on his chest to be a galloping horse to cellophane he could crumple for a fire.

"One day we had a play that called for the sound of water falling on a board. Well, during rehearsal the poor fellow tried everything — rice on a drum, dried peas on cardboard — but nothing would give him the sound of water on a board.

"Finally, one day he tried water on a board, and you know, it sounded just like water on a board."

～

One of the things Reagan did as a radio announcer was to broadcast baseball games. Reagan worked with a man named Curly, who would listen to the play-by-play come in on the telegraph wire. Curly would type out what was happening and slip the paper to Reagan, who would then announce the play on the radio. Most of the time this arrangement worked well, but occasionally there would be a mishap:

"On this summer's day the Cubs and the St. Louis Cards were locked in a scoreless tie: Dizzy Dean on the mound, Augie Galan at bat for the Cubs in the ninth inning. I saw Curly start to type, so I finished the windup and had Dean send the ball on its way to the plate, took the slip from Curly, and found myself faced with the terse note: 'The wire has gone dead.'

"I had a ball on the way to the plate, and there was no way to call it back. At the same time, I was convinced that a ball game tied up in the ninth inning was no time to tell my audience we had lost contact with the game and they would have to listen to recorded music. I knew of only one thing that wouldn't get in the score column and betray me — a foul ball. So I had Augie foul this pitch down the left-field foul line. I looked expectantly at Curly. He just shrugged helplessly, so I had Augie foul another one, and still another; then he fouled one back into the box seats. I described in detail the redheaded kid who had scrambled and gotten the souvenir ball. He fouled one into the upper deck that just missed being a home run. He fouled for six minutes and forty-five seconds, until I lost count. I began to be frightened that maybe I was establishing a new world record for a fellow staying at bat hitting fouls, and this could betray me. Yet I was into it so far I didn't dare reveal that the wire had gone dead. My voice was rising in pitch and threatening to crack — and then, bless him, Curly started typing. I clutched at the slip. It said: 'Galan popped out on the first ball pitched.' Not in my game he didn't — he popped out after practically making a career of foul balls."

~

When he was living in Des Moines, Reagan stopped an armed robbery:

"I was half awake and heard some voices raised. I thought it was a marital fight or some kind of couple having a quarrel. I heard an angry tone and then a woman's voice saying, 'Take everything I've got, but let me go.' In about a second and a half I was at the window. My apartment was on the second floor. He was standing there with a gun on her. She had a suitcase at her side. I've always had some guns around, and I started for one on the mantel and then realized that I didn't have any bullets and it wouldn't do any good up there in the dark to have an empty gun, although it might if I was down there with him. So I just went back to the window. Knowing he couldn't see into the dark where I was, I said, 'Drop it and get going or I'm going to blow your head off. I've got a .45 up here.' He turned around and pointed the gun up and realized that he couldn't see me in the dark. I yelled, 'Drop it!' and all of a sudden he took off and ran."

~

In 1937 Reagan talked the radio station into sending him to Catalina, California, to cover the Chicago Cubs training session there. In his free time, Reagan had screen tests at Warner Brothers and Paramount. His first day back in Des Moines, Reagan received a telegram: It said: WARNER'S OFFER CONTRACT SEVEN YEARS, ONE YEAR'S OPTIONS, STARTING AT $200 A WEEK. WHAT SHALL I DO? The message was from Bill Meiklejohn, his agent.

Reagan replied: SIGN BEFORE THEY CHANGE THEIR MINDS.

The Hollywood Years

In 1937 Ronald Reagan arrived in Hollywood, an unmarried Democrat who had never been too involved in politics. When he left in 1966, he was a married father of four running for governor of California on the Republican ticket. However, his wit and love for a good story did not change.

During his remarks at a White House ceremony honoring the National Teacher of the Year on April 9, 1984:

"It was a teacher who steered me into acting, an English teacher named B. J. Fraser, back in Dixon, Illinois. He's gone now, but I can somehow imagine him saying, 'But I take no responsibility for his going into politics.'"

~

Reagan said the film that most affected his life was *Mr. Smith Goes to Washington:*

"When Jimmy Stewart walked the halls of the Capitol building, I walked with him. When he stood in awe of that great man at the Lincoln Memorial, I bowed my head too. When he stood in the Senate chamber and refused to knuckle under to the vested interests, I began to realize, through the power of motion pictures, that one man can make a difference."

∽

The first movie Warner Brothers cast Reagan in kept the novice movie actor close to what he already knew:

"Maybe it wasn't intentional, but my first role at Warner Brothers sure seemed like typecasting: I was assigned to play a radio announcer in a movie initially called *Inside Story,* then renamed *Love Is on the Air.* It was a typical B movie — made in a hurry and forgettable.

"My preparations for the part consisted of a day with a dialogue coach; at least it was a day longer than the preparation I'd had for my radio announcer's job in [Iowa]. The coach went over the script with me and told me to report for work the next day.

"When I woke up the following morning, I wanted to get out of town as quickly as I could. I thought about getting in my car and driving non-stop to Iowa.

"Nothing I'd ever experienced — no stage fright before a college show or steeplechase jump or dive from a high platform, nothing I'd been through, had ever produced in me the kind of jitters I felt when I stepped onto Stage Eight at Warner Brothers that morning.

"'Kid, don't worry,' a veteran actor who was in my first scene said. 'Just take it easy and everything will be all right.'

"They sponged some makeup on my face, I took my place on the set, the lights went on, and the director, Nick Grinde, said: 'Camera . . . Action.'

"Suddenly, my jitters were gone. The old character actor had been right.

As soon as I heard the director's words, I forgot all about the camera and the lights and the crew and concentrated on delivering my lines in a way that I hoped would make B. J. Fraser proud.

"A couple of minutes later, the director said, 'Cut.' To my amazement, he said he was satisfied with the first take. He started setting up to shoot the next scene, and I sat down on one of those canvas chairs you see on movie sets (without my name on it) and said silently to myself: *You know, maybe I can make it here.*

~

In *Knute Rockne — All American,* Reagan was in the picture for only a few minutes, but it contained one of his most memorable lines:

"Just before Gipp died, I said to Rockne: 'Someday when things are tough and the breaks are going against the boys, ask them to go in there and win one for the Gipper. I don't know where I'll be, but I'll know about it and I'll be happy.'"

~

Reagan recalled the audience's reaction to his line:

"As I spoke these words, men and women in the audience started pulling out their handkerchiefs. Then, from the back to the front of the theater, I heard sniffles, making me wonder if this was the breakthrough I'd been waiting for."

~

Reagan did start getting more leading roles after *Knute,* but he was always hoping to get away from being typecast:

"[When] I was making pictures, I had a running battle with Warner Brothers. I was under contract there for thirteen years, and they had me in the light-drawing-room-comedy-type pictures simply because if you are in one that makes money, you're typecast from then on. They were successful pictures, but I wanted to do more outdoor pictures. I wanted to play the Errol Flynn–type role. I remember in an argument with Jack Warner about this, I got furious, and finally I blurted out, 'If you ever do put me in a Western, you'll make me the lawyer from the East.'"

∾

Reagan was married to actress Jane Wyman from 1940 to 1948. Other than to say, "The marriage produced two wonderful children, Maureen and Michael," he has never said much about it publicly. In *Where's the Rest of Me?*, an autobiography, Reagan made perhaps his most expansive statement on this part of his life:

"Jane Wyman and I met in 1939, making *Brother Rat*. We became engaged during a cross-country tour with Louella Parsons who, incidentally, came from my hometown. Louella took a group of us on a nine weeks' vaudeville tour as her picks for future stardom. She picked pretty good too: June Preisser, Susan Hayward, Joy Hodges, Arlene Whelan, Jane, and me. I think I could interject that through all that followed, Louella remained scrupulously fair and grieved [at the divorce], as she always does when fate knocks some of us Hollywoodians kicking. We may be grist for the newspaper mill, but we are also friends in her book and the only way we can lose that is if we 'betray the industry.'

"Divorce happens in every town, but somehow people reserve a special feeling for it when it happens in [Hollywood]. I think that some of our less stable (and they are a very small percentage) glamour peddlers with a frequent repeat pattern have given the public impression that it isn't tragic here — that no one takes it seriously. That, of course, isn't true: if you hit us we bruise, if you cut us (forgive me, Shakespeare) we bleed. When we have a domestic problem, we can't tackle it in any atmosphere of privacy. I have never discussed what happened, and I have no intention of doing so now.

"The problem hurt our children most. Maureen was born in 1941 and Michael came to us in March of 1945 — closer than a son; he wasn't born unasked, we chose him. There is no easy way to break up a home, and I don't think there is any way to ease the bewildered pain of children at such times."

∼

In Reagan's autobiography *Where's the Rest of Me?* he writes about *King's Row,* which was the highlight of his film career:

"I rehearsed the scene before mirrors, in corners of the studio, while driving home, in the men's room of restaurants, before selected friends. At night I would wake up staring at the ceiling and automatically mutter the line before I went back to sleep. I consulted physicians and psychologists; I even talked to people who were so disabled, trying to brew in myself the cauldron of emotions a man must feel who wakes up one sunny morning to find half of himself gone."

∼

Reagan said during his remarks on signing a World Trade Week proclamation on May 5, 1986:

"In those days American motion pictures occupied more than seventy-five percent of the playing time of all the screens in the world. Unfortunately, the movies that we sent overseas sometimes — well, they weren't always successful. I had one called *Cattle Queen of Montana.* It lost something in Japanese."

⁓

Some of the challenges Reagan faced on the job in Hollywood were between takes:

"I did a string of pictures with the Dead End Kids, which was an experience similar to going over Niagara Falls in a barrel the hard way — upstream. Counting noses and getting them all in one scene was a major chore, but sometimes it was a relief when they did take off and disappear for a few hours. You never knew when a canvas chair would go up in smoke, or be blown apart by the giant firecrackers they were never without. Having heard lurid tales from other actors, I approached my first picture with them in something of a sweat. Jimmy Cagney solved my problem one noon at the corner table. Having had his beginnings in the same New York Hell's Kitchen, he understood these kids as no one else could. 'It's very simple,' he said. 'Just tell them you look forward to working with them, but you'll slap hell out of them if they do one thing out of line.' He was right — it was just that simple. I had the only unscorched chair on the set."

⁓

Of another movie, Reagan writes:

"One big action scene involved a gang fight with goons smashing up a truckload of tomatoes. For three nights we wallowed around in those tomatoes — the same tomatoes. By the third night the prop men were scooping them up with shovels and slopping them back into crates for the next shot. At midnight we called a halt for lunch, our clothes plastered with wet squashed tomatoes, so that no one felt like putting on a coat or sweater over the mess in spite of the cold night air. Suddenly there was a roar of anger from the first men in line, who happened to be stuntmen. The next thing we knew, a frightened caterer was sprinting out into the darkness across the tomato field with six burly stuntmen after him. The damned fool was serving stewed tomatoes."

~

Reflecting on what is involved in being in Hollywood, Reagan told his daughter Maureen that she had to continue her education, "because you have to be able to sign contracts and give autographs," and because "you will have to be able to read scripts." Maureen used to tell this story as a way of showing how her father charmed children.

~

Reagan served in the United States Army Air Corps from 1942–1945. He was a captain. This funny moment was one of his first in the military:

"Colonel Ferguson turned me over to the adjunct at Fort Mason on the first day of my military service. I discovered that even though I was in, another physical was required. I went through the same old business with the eyes, and one of the two examining doctors said, 'If you went overseas, you'd shoot a general.'

"The other doctor looked up and said, 'Yes, and you'd miss him.'"

~

Reagan was not the only Hollywood star to serve his country during World War II:

"I have a story, and I hope that Jimmy Stewart won't object to my repeating it.

"He would introduce me at various banquets along the campaign trail, and every time the emcee introduced him, he would talk about his great stardom in the pictures.

"Each time I got up, I would apologize to the emcee for correcting him and add about Jimmy's war record that he not only flew the Hamburg run, but that he was a major general in the Air Corps Reserve.

"One time, after several of these situations, the master of ceremonies did refer to Jimmy's military record and then said, 'Brigadier General Jimmy Stewart.' So when I got up, I apologized to the emcee once again and said, 'It's Major General Jimmy Stewart.'

"That night when we got back to the hotel, Jimmy said, 'Ron, that fellow was right — it is brigadier general. I just never corrected you before because it sounded so good.'"

❧

In 1947, Reagan was elected to the first of his six terms as president of the Screen Actors Guild. Many years later he was asked how this experience helped prepare him for his life in politics:

"For two decades I participated in the negotiations of the basic contract with the producers. We had a test: is it good for the actors, is it fair to the other fellow, and is it good for the industry? If we couldn't answer yes to those three things about an issue, we didn't raise that issue.

"Then, during the mid-forties, communists were fighting for control of the film unions and guilds. There were threats of violence against guild members, and against me personally. It was then I learned something that kind of set the stage for me as governor, and, later on, here. There couldn't help but be times when I said to myself, 'Who am I to be making decisions for thousands of actors whose careers are at stake?' I finally decided the only way I could sleep at night was if I did what I honestly believed was right. I might make a mistake, but that was what we'd do. And with that rule, I do sleep very well."

~

Of course Nancy Davis, who would become Nancy Reagan and go with Ronald when he moved on to Sacramento and later Washington, merits more than a mere mention — which is why she has a section dedicated solely to her later in the book. However, it is appropriate to mention her here because Reagan did meet her in Hollywood, and the story of how they met not only says a lot about each of them and their relationship, but it paints a picture of what the atmosphere was like in Hollywood at this time. They met because another actress named Nancy Davis had been identified as a member of a number of organizations known as fronts for the Communist Party. Such affiliations damaged more than one promising Hollywood career, and the future Mrs. Reagan wanted to make sure her name was in the clear. The director Mervyn LeRoy got in touch with Reagan, who was then president of the Screen Actors Guild, and asked him to look into it. Reagan sent his assurances that she was in the clear through LeRoy, who said the actress should hear it from Reagan himself. "She's a worrier." Reagan agreed to do this.

"To be on the safe side, however, when I called her, I said: 'I have an early call in the morning, so I'm afraid we'll have to make it an early evening.'

"'Fine,' Nancy said, 'I've got an early call too. I can't stay out too late, either.'

"She had her pride too.

"We were both lying."

They discussed the original problem at hand, but soon moved on to other subjects.

"Although we'd agreed to call it an early night, I didn't want the evening to end, so I said: 'Have you ever seen Sophie Tucker? She's singing at Ciro's, just down the street. Why don't we go see the first show?'

"Well, she'd never heard Sophie Tucker before, so we went to Ciro's to catch the first show. Then we stayed for the second show, and we got home at about three o'clock in the morning. No mention was made of early calls."

∽

In 1954, Reagan became the host of "General Electric Theater," a very popular television show at the time. His responsibilities included being the spokesman for the company's personnel program. He recalls that the experience was not just "shaking hands, but talking to workers and listening to what was on their minds":

"Looking back now, I realize it wasn't a bad apprenticeship for someone who'd someday enter public life — although, believe me, that was the farthest thing from my mind in those days."

∽

"I've met so many people in my life that whenever I encounter someone, I have to assume I might have met that person previously. Before committing myself, I sort of look for clues and react accordingly — although sometimes that technique backfires. Once back in my Hollywood days, a man came up to me in the lobby of the Plaza Hotel in New York, stuck out his hand, and said, 'You don't know me . . .' So many people did that to me that I just said, 'Wait a minute, oh sure I do, I'm just trying to remember . . .'" He said, 'No, you *don't* know me, I just wanted to tell you how much I enjoy your television program.'"

~

Reagan said the following about the acting career:

"So much of [the] profession is taken up with pretending, with the interpretation of never-never roles, that an actor must spend at least half his waking hours in fantasy, in rehearsal or shooting. If he is only an actor, I feel, he was much like I was in *King's Row,* only half a man — no matter how great his talents. I regard acting with the greatest affection; it has made my life for me. But I realize it tends to become an island of exaggerated importance. During my career on the screen I have commanded excellent salaries, some admiration, fan mail, and a reputation — and my world contracted into not much more than a sound stage, my home, and occasional nights on the town. The circle of my friends closed in. The demands of my work — sometimes as much as fourteen hours a day — cut me off even from my brother, Neil, who lived within half a mile of my apartment."

~

It was during his Hollywood years that Reagan switched from the Democratic Party to the Republican:

"I can tell you how traumatic it was when it actually came down to reregistering and saying, 'I am a member of another party.' I talked myself into it.

"When I voted in 1932 for Franklin Delano Roosevelt, the Democratic platform pledged a twenty-five percent cut in federal spending, and he campaigned on a return of authority to the people who had lost it to the government. I went on and was a loyal Democrat. But on the mashed-potato circuit I began to talk more and more about how government had expanded and was infringing on liberties and interfering with private enterprise. One day I came home from a speaking tour and I said to Nancy, 'I go out there and make these speeches, which I believe, and then every four years I find myself campaigning for the people who are doing the things I'm speaking against.' And I said, 'I'm on the wrong side.'"

~

In retrospect, Reagan said, acting made him realize what other aspects of himself he had yet to seek:

"Possibly this was the reason I decided to find the rest of me. I love three things: drama, politics, and sports, and I'm not sure they always come in that order. In all three of them I came out of the monastery of movies into the world. In sports, though I could no longer play top football, I could still swim or ride horseback or simply watch. In motion pictures or television, I could do more than a competent job. In politics, I found myself in the middle of the biggest tohubohu of my life."

GOVERNOR

Some would say that the switch from actor to politician is unnatural, but it definitely felt like a natural progression to Reagan, who had become increasingly active politically while he was in Hollywood. Whatever doubts the skeptics had, Reagan appeased enough of them to win two terms in office as governor and become a player on the national political scene.

Campaign for Governor

On January 1, 1966, Ronald Reagan announced his candidacy for the Republican nomination for governor of California. He beat former San Francisco mayor George Christopher in the primary and faced incumbent Democrat Edmund G. (Pat) Brown in the general election.

When he first ran for the office in 1966, Reagan was asked what kind of governor he would make. Reagan replied, "I don't know, I've never played a governor."

~

Reagan, with no political-office background, but rather an acting one, was well aware of the stereotype he faced going into public service:

"Still, I realized that if I didn't handle this right, the 'he's only an actor' theme could hurt me. I knew a lot of people had misconceptions about actors: If you're an actor, the only thing you can do is act. . . . Yes, you've played a lot of parts on the screen, but it's only make-believe and that's *all* you can do: pretend. . . . Those who can, do; those who can't, act."

~

Reagan remembered much later:

"You know, years ago, when the news first came out that I was running for governor of California, someone asked my boss Jack Warner what he thought of the idea. And it's been reported to me that Warner said, 'No, no. Jimmy Stewart for governor; Reagan for best friend.'"

~

Accusations were made about Reagan not writing his own speeches during the campaign. Reagan had an idea to prove his sincerity. He said to his campaign managers Stu Spencer and Bill Roberts:

"From now on, why don't I just say a few words to whatever group I'm with, no matter how big it is, and then just open it up to questions and answers? People might think somebody had written my opening remarks for me, but they'll know it would be impossible for somebody to feed me answers to questions I didn't know about in advance."

Reagan said later:

"The political professionals in our group blanched when I said that. They were used to hiding candidates, not turning them loose."

~

In retrospect of his 1966 California gubernatorial victory:

"In different ways, the election changed the lives of everyone in our family that night."

Eight Years in Office

Reagan originally "fought like a tiger against ever running for office," but once he was in office he said, "I have to tell you, we'd only been in the governor's mansion a few months, and one night [Nancy and I] looked at each other, sitting in the living room in Sacramento, and said, 'This makes everything else we've done look as dull as dishwater.'"

Reagan said that although the first year in Sacramento was very difficult, he and Nancy had learned a lot:

"For years, I'd been giving speeches about the problems in government. Now, after being dragged kicking and screaming into public office at a time when the state was facing a real emergency and uncovering problems I hadn't even known existed before, I'd been given a chance to do something about them."

∾

Before presenting his first state budget, Reagan said:

"What I have recently learned about the state of finances in California [means] we may turn out to be the first state that ever ran on Diner's Club cards."

Once Governor Reagan had to change his tune on a tax increase. He had said that his feet were set in cement when it came to raising taxes. Reagan then told a press conference:

"Ladies and gentlemen, the sound you hear is the concrete beginning to crack around my feet."

~

Reagan was governor during the Vietnam War. He had strong opinions about stopping the spread of communism:

"Isn't it time that we admitted we are in Vietnam because our national interest demands that we take a stand there now so we won't have to take a stand later on our own beaches? Isn't it time that we either win this war or tell the American people why we can't?"

~

Student riots were a common occurrence in the public university system in California during this time. However, Reagan worked at finding common ground with the student leaders:

"I was governor of California back in the riotous days of the sixties. And I couldn't go to a college football game. There'd be a riot instead. Anyone in authority was in the same position. But I remember one day when a group of the leaders of that came from the campuses of the University of California to Sacramento. They had demanded a meeting with me. Well, I was delighted because, as I say, I couldn't go and meet with them.

"So they came in and, as was the custom of the day of that particular group of young people, they were barefoot, and wore torn T-shirts, and slouched in their chairs. And finally one of them who was the spokesman said to me, 'Governor, it's impossible for you to understand us.' And I tried to pass it off. I said, 'Well, we know more about being young than we do about being old.' And he said, 'No, your generation cannot understand their own sons and daughters.' He said, 'You didn't grow up in an era of computers figuring in seconds what it used to take men years to figure out.' And he went on like that. And usually you only think of the answer after you're gone, but the Lord was good to me. And he talked long enough that I finally interrupted him, and I said, 'Wait a minute. It's true what you said. We didn't grow up, my generation, with those things. We invented them.'"

~

Many were pushing for the legalization of drugs, especially marijuana, while Reagan was governor. Reagan held a firm line, foreshadowing the stand Nancy would take years later when she led the "Just Say No" campaign:

"I am opposed [to the legalization of marijuana]. And I am opposed because the score is not in yet [on the medical effects of its use]. The thing I think most people don't realize about legalization of marijuana is that fourteen companies have already registered trademarks for marijuana cigarettes. Once you make them legal, you're going to see billboards, and packs in the vending machines. Since marijuana is smoked for effect — not for the taste as cigarettes — how are they going to advertise? What are they going to say — 'Fly higher with ours'?"

~

At the National Association of Student Councils Reagan said the following about government paperwork and bureaucracy:

"I know of a teacher who realized one day that the form he kept getting, kept filling out, and kept sending in, asked some of the same questions over and over again, such as what was the size of his classroom.

"He got curious as to whether anybody in Washington ever read those reports, so each time he filled out the same old form, he increased the size of his classroom until he got to the size of the Coliseum. But there was no protest from Washington.

"Then he went the other way. He started reducing it so that his classroom was smaller than a steamer trunk, and still there was no word from Washington. That's when he decided, 'Why fill them out? No one's reading them.'

"This is the type of excess bureaucracy we can do without."

～

One time during Reagan's years as governor, he had an embarrassing moment while speaking in Mexico City:

"After I had finished, I sat down to rather unenthusiastic applause, and I was a little embarrassed.

"The speaker who followed me spoke in Spanish — which I didn't understand — and he was being applauded about every paragraph.

"To hide my embarrassment I started clapping before everyone else and longer than anyone else until our ambassador leaned over and said, 'I wouldn't do that if I were you; he's interpreting your speech.'"

～

During Thanksgiving when Reagan was governor, turkey growers used to bring in a cooked turkey for him to carve, and he would have lunch right there with his staff in the office:

"But I had to carve it for all those ladies and gentlemen of the press with their cameras on me.

"I remember one day I was carving, and I thought they hadn't cooked it very well because there was quite a bit of blood appearing, which didn't look too appetizing.

"I found out I'd cut my thumb. Sort of spoiled lunch."

～

As governor, Reagan made an effort to comfort people struck by natural disasters and to see for himself the areas that had been damaged. He was often struck by the strength and composure of those affected by these disasters:

"We had experienced heavy rains, and so I visited an area in Santa Barbara where there had been great mud slides. I was there to see what the damage was and how we could be of help to forestall this from happening in the future.

"An elderly gentleman of Mexican descent motioned to me to come into his home. And there we stood in the wreckage of what had been his living room, both of us knee-deep in muddy water.

"And with the greatest dignity he said to me, '*Mi casa es su casa.*'"

～

Toward the end of his second term, Reagan said of being governor:

"There are some days you go home so frustrated that you get in the shower and you make speeches to the walls of the shower. But there are other days when you go home and feel ten feet tall because you have solved a problem."

THE PRESIDENCY

When Reagan ran for President in the 1980 campaign, the country had gone through a period of rapid inflation and an oil crisis, and American hostages had been held in Iran for almost a year. A feeling of discontent was prevalent in the United States at the time, and Reagan, with his vision, faith, and, of course, charm, gave people a sense of hope. He gave them faith that the country could renew itself and become once again the country of the American Dream.

Campaigns

Late in the 1980 campaign Reagan summed up the sentiment of his entire campaign in one brief, eloquent statement:

"If not us, then who? If not now, when?"

～

Reagan felt that the American people had been stifled by a large federal government that interfered with rather than promoted progress:

"This idea that government was beholden to the people, that it had no other source of power, is still the newest, most unique idea in all the long history of man's relation to man. This is the issue of this election: whether we believe in our capacity for self-government or whether we abandon the American Revolution and confess that a little intellectual elite in a far-distant capital can plan our lives for us better than we can plan them ourselves."

≈

Reagan said this of his opponent, President Jimmy Carter:

"Recession is when your neighbor loses his job. Depression is when you lose yours. And recovery is when Jimmy Carter loses his."

≈

"I can't do a damn thing for you unless I'm elected."

≈

"I would never accuse our political opponents of ignorance. It's just that there are so many people in Washington who know so many things that aren't true."

≈

In *Speaking My Mind,* Reagan made the following remark about the 1984 presidential campaign:

"I don't know why, but during the '84 campaign the audiences seemed to get caught up in the spirit of things, and they'd start chanting or yelling things out to me. It was really quite a party, a Republican party as things turned out."

≈

A member of Reagan's staff once asked him if he could feel the audience's adulation. Reagan said he could:

"In fact, I bet I have a better idea of what it feels like to be a rock star than most twenty-year-olds."

∽

When asked how he handled enthusiasm like that he found on the campaign trail, Reagan said:

"I pray I will be deserving. I always tried to remember that; otherwise the power goes to your head, and the history books are littered with such unsavory people."

∽

At a rally for Senator Mark Andrews in Grand Forks, North Dakota, on September 17, 1986, Reagan received repeated chants of "Four more years" from the audience. He replied:

"Thank you very much. And since the Constitution has something to say about what you've just been chanting, I'll assume that you're suggesting that I live for four more years."

∽

When he ran in 1984, Reagan had the advantage of having a presidential track record he could point to:

"Are you better off than you were four years ago? Is it easier for you to go and buy things in the stores than it was four years ago? Is there more or less employment in the country than there was four years ago? Is America respected throughout the world as it was? Do you feel that our security is as safe, that we're as strong as we were four years ago? And if you answer all those questions 'Yes,' why I think your choice is very obvious as to who you'll vote for. If you don't think this course we've been on for the last four years is what you would like to see us follow for the next four, then I could suggest another choice that you have."

~

Naturally, when opponents tried to make Reagan's age a negative, he turned the argument around:

"I want you to know that also I will not make age an issue of this campaign. I am not going to exploit, for political purposes, my opponent's youth and inexperience."

~

During the 1984 campaign, Reagan was asked how it felt to be running his last campaign for public office:

"Well, there can't help but be some relief in that. Because it's a hard road. I only had one previous experience of running as an incumbent, where you've got to do the job as well as campaign. And I have to tell you, being the challenger is a lot easier."

The First Term

Sometimes the most significant moments in our lives happen when we are least expecting them:

"Late that afternoon, I was in the shower, getting cleaned up for the evening, when Nancy, who'd already taken her bath and was wrapped in a towel, came into the bathroom and shouted above the drizzle of the shower that I was wanted on the telephone. 'It's Jimmy Carter,' she said. I turned off the water and got out of the shower and dried off a little, then grabbed an extension phone in the bathroom while Nancy stood beside me. After listening for a few minutes, I said, 'Thank you, Mr. President.' Then I hung up the phone and looked at Nancy and said, 'He conceded. He said he wanted to congratulate me.' Instinctively, she gave me a big hug and I hugged her. The polls in California wouldn't even close for another two hours. But standing in my bathroom with a towel wrapped around me, my hair dripping with water, I had just learned I was going to be the fortieth President of the United States."

∾

Before the inauguration, a reporter asked Reagan, "Are you thinking of a phrase to explain what it [America] is about?"

Reagan answered, "Maybe it's contained in the slogan for the inauguration itself: 'America, A New Beginning.' . . . I want to go in a different direction. I want to depend on the vitality and the strength of the people of this country when they're in the system the way I believe it was intended to be run, when their abilities are unleashed and there is incentive for them to go out and try to do better. I want to reduce the cost of government, reduce the part it plays in the people's lives, not in a destructive way, but in a way that takes away the hobbles that we have put on business, industry, and the individual. I happen to believe it. Why don't we try it?"

∾

Reagan's chief of staff Michael Deaver walked into the President's room on the morning of the inauguration at about 9 A.M. Deaver told Reagan, "You're going to be inaugurated in two hours."

Reagan replied, "Does that mean I have to get up?"

~

In his First Inaugural Address, on January 20, 1981, Reagan said:

"No arsenal or no weapon in the arsenals of the world is so formidable as the will and moral courage of free men and women."

~

Reagan said of himself as he began to serve his first term as President of the United States:

"If I could do this, I thought, then truly any child in America had an opportunity to do it."

~

However, Reagan had a little help behind the scenes:

"They tell me I'm the most powerful man in the world. I don't believe that. Over there at the White House someplace there's a fellow that puts a piece of paper on my desk every day that tells me what I'm going to do every fifteen minutes. He's the most powerful man in the world."

~

Reagan was asked by friends what surprised him the most about the White House:

"The biggest surprises are the leaks. I'll tell you, I've gotten so that I address some things in cabinet meetings to the chandelier. I'm sure it must have a microphone."

~

Reagan soon learned the advantages of his new job. When asked by a supporter if he liked being President better than being a movie actor, Reagan answered:

"Yes, because here I get to write the script too."

~

During the early months of Reagan's presidency, he and his staff spent a lot of time discussing appointments to key jobs in the administration:

"As I had done in California, I told the staff I wanted them to look for the best people we could find who were willing to leave their homes and their secure positions to come to Washington and give the country a hand. When I'd approach somebody about taking a job, I'd often say, "We don't want people who *want* a job in government, we want people of accomplishment who have to be *persuaded* to come to work here.""

~

Reagan mapped out a clear agenda during his 1980 campaign, focusing on the economy and on reining in big government. However, it wasn't until he got to Washington that he realized how big a job that was going to be:

"I remember John Kennedy saying that when he came into office, the thing that surprised him the most was to find that things were just as bad as he'd been saying they were. In my case, the biggest surprise was finding out that they were even worse. And it's a real human tragedy that so many of our people today are still suffering from the political mistakes of the past that we've finally started to correct."

~

Reagan brought his faith in the American people to the White House with him:

"There are no such things as limits to growth, because there are no limits on the human capacity for intelligence, imagination, and wonder."

The Assassination Attempt

On March 30, 1981, after Reagan had been in office for only three months, John W. Hinckley, Jr., tried to assassinate the President as he left the Washington, D.C., Hilton Hotel. James S. Brady, the President's press secretary, was shot in the head; Secret Service agent Timothy J. McCarthy was shot in the chest, and policeman Thomas K. Delahanty was shot in the neck. The President was hit when a bullet ricocheted off the limousine. The bullet entered the President's body under his left arm and came within an inch of his heart. Thankfully, all four men lived. When Reagan left the hospital and returned to the White House, he wrote in his diary, "Whatever happens now, I owe my life to God and will try to serve Him in every way I can."

~

Everything happened so fast that at the time, Reagan did not realize that an attempt had been made on his life:

"I was almost to the car when I heard what sounded like two or three firecrackers over to my left — just a small fluttering sound, *pop, pop, pop.*

"I turned and said, 'What the hell's that?'

"Just then, Jerry Parr, the head of our Secret Service, grabbed me by the waist and literally hurled me into the back of the limousine. I landed on my face atop the armrest across the backseat and Jerry jumped on top of me. When he landed, I felt a pain in my upper back that was unbelievable. It was the most excruciating pain I had ever felt.

"'Jerry,' I said, 'get off, I think you've broken one of my ribs.'

"'The White House,' Jerry told the driver, then scrambled off me and got on the jump seat and the car took off.

"I tried to sit up on the edge of the seat and was almost paralyzed by pain. As I was straightening up, I had to cough hard and saw that the palm of my hand was brimming with extremely red, frothy blood.

"'You not only broke a rib, I think the rib punctured my lung,' I said.

"Jerry looked at the bubbles of blood and told the driver to head for George Washington University Hospital instead of the White House.

"By then my handkerchief was sopped with blood, and he handed me his. Suddenly, I realized I could barely breathe. No matter how hard I tried, I couldn't get enough air. I was frightened and started to panic a little. I just was not able to inhale enough air.

"We pulled up in front of the hospital emergency room. A nurse was coming to meet me, and I told her I was having trouble breathing. Then all of a sudden my knees turned rubbery. The next thing I knew, I was lying face up on a gurney and my brand-new pin-striped suit was being cut off me, never to be worn again."

~

At the annual dinner of the White House Correspondents' Association in 1981, Reagan, who made his remarks by telephone, said:

"If I could just give you one little bit of advice, when somebody tells you to get in a car quick, do it."

~

To the hospital staff upon entering the hospital, Reagan said in reference to John Hinckley:

"Does anybody know what that guy's beef was?"

~

Even when he first arrived in the hospital, unsure of how serious his condition was, Reagan maintained a sense of humor. He quipped to doctors as he was taken to surgery:

"Please tell me you're a Republican."

~

He also said to his wife:

"Honey, I forgot to duck."

~

To daughter Maureen by telephone after the operation on March 30, 1981:

"The bullet ruined one of my best suits."

Reagan paraphrased Winston Churchill:

"There is no more exhilarating feeling than being shot at without result."

∽

One of Reagan's most vivid memories of his time in the hospital is of an anonymous guardian angel, who offered comfort at just the right moment.

"I was lying on the gurney only half conscious when I realized that some-one was holding my hand. It was a soft, feminine hand. I felt it come up and touch mine and then hold on tight to it. It gave me a wonderful feel-ing. Even now I find it difficult to explain how reassuring, how wonderful, it felt.

"It must have been the hand of a nurse kneeling very close to the gurney, but I couldn't see her. I started asking, 'Who's holding my hand? . . . Who's holding my hand?' When I didn't hear any response, I said, 'Does Nancy know about us?'

"Although I tried afterward to learn who the nurse was, I was never able to find her. I wanted to tell her how much the touch of her hand had meant to me, but I never was able to do that."

∽

Reagan was treated very well at the George Washington University Hospi-tal. The medical staff was attentive and helped keep the President in good spirits. He told them:

"If I had this much attention in Hollywood, I'd have stayed there."

∽

When Lyn Nofziger rushed into the hospital to tell his wounded boss that everything in Washington was "running normally," Reagan replied, "What makes you think I'd be happy about that?"

~

The President greatly appreciated the letters of support and well-wishing he received from all over the country. In an address before a joint session of the Congress on the Program for Economic Recovery on April 28, one month after the assassination attempt, Reagan shared one of these letters:

"I have a letter with me. The letter came from Peter Sweeney. He's in the second grade in the Riverside School in Rockville Center, and he said, 'I hope you get well quick or you might have to make a speech in your pajamas.' He added a postscript. 'P.S. If you have to make a speech in your pajamas, I warned you.'"

Reagan also felt the power of the country's prayers:

"It's a remarkable feeling to know that people are praying for you and for your strength. I know firsthand. I felt those prayers when I was recovering from that bullet."

~

Reagan was happy to resume his presidential duties, busy schedule and all. During his remarks at the Santa-Cali-Gon-Days celebration in Independence, Missouri, on September 2, 1985, he said:

"Now this is the first time I've really been out on the stump since I was in the hospital, and I missed doing this. I missed it. I even miss hecklers."

In a 1990 interview on the "Larry King Live" show, Reagan said he had forgiven John Hinckley, who was found innocent by reason of insanity of trying to assassinate the President in 1981:

"I found out he wasn't thinking on all cylinders."

The assassination attempt did not change the President's view on gun control:

"My position has always been clear — I believe that law-abiding citizens have a right to bear arms. I believe, too, that within that right comes a responsibility to use guns safely and in compliance with the law. . . .

"So I believe, as I've said before, that we should concentrate on increasing the penalties for those who use guns to commit crime."

∾

Reagan did not feel that tougher gun control laws would have prevented the attempt on his life:

"It's a nasty truth, but those who seek to inflict harm are not fazed by gun controllers. I happen to know this from personal experience."

∾

Reagan was speaking before the Building and Construction Trades Department of the AFL–CIO just before the attempt on his life in 1981. One year later he returned to address the same group:

"I know you all understand how happy I am to be back — standing before you today. If it's all the same to you, though, when I finish speaking, I think I'll slip out the back door this time."

A few years later, while the President was making a speech, a popped balloon created a panic, but the President kept his cool:

"We can make America stronger, not just economically and militarily, but also morally and spiritually. We can make our beloved country the source of all the dreams and the opportunities that she was —
   [At this point, a balloon popped in the arena, sounding like a gunshot.]
"Missed me . . ."

The Economy

Reagan made the economy one of the top priorities of his first term. He fought against those who wanted to raise taxes. Reagan believed that taxpayers had the right to keep more of what they earned, and that left in their hands, the money was more likely to stimulate the economy. He said quite simply, "This Administration's objective will be a healthy, vigorous, growing economy."

He said in a speech on September 29, 1981:

"We who live in free market societies believe that growth, prosperity, and ultimately human fulfillment are created from the bottom up, not the government down. Only when the human spirit is allowed to invent and create, only when individuals are given a personal stake in deciding economic policies and benefiting from their success — only then can societies remain economically alive, dynamic, progressive, and free. Trust the people. This is the one irrefutable lesson of the entire postwar period, contradicting the notion that rigid government controls are essential to economic development."

~

Reagan had it clear in his mind what the test of his economic program would be:

"Government has an important role in helping develop a country's economic foundation. But the critical test is whether government is genuinely working to liberate individuals by creating incentives to work, save, invest, and succeed."

~

During Reagan's address to the National Association of Realtors, March 28, 1982, he said:

"We don't have a trillion-dollar debt because we haven't taxed enough; we have a trillion-dollar debt because we spend too much."

~

Despite the skepticism of his critics, Reagan stuck by his economic plan:

"We've put in place an economic program that is based on sound economic theory, not political expediency. We will not play hopscotch economics, jumping here and there as the daily situation changes."

~

Reagan challenged his critics who didn't offer an alternative plan:

"To the paid political complainers, let me say as politely as I can, 'Put up or shut up.'"

~

During his campaign and the early days of his administration, Reagan's critics mocked his economic plan, calling it "Reaganomics." When the economy showed signs of recovery, they changed their tune:

"One of the best signs that our economic program is working is that they don't call it Reaganomics anymore."

~

Reagan often used this story to illustrate some of the problems with certain economic theories:

"A man knocked on his neighbor's door and asked, 'Do you own a black pit bull?'

"The neighbor said that he did, and the man who knocked on the door said: 'My Pekinese killed it.'

"'Your Pekinese killed it?' the neighbor responded incredulously. 'How?'

"'It got stuck in his throat.'"

~

Even an issue as serious as the economy was not exempt from Reagan's witty commentary:

"Once upon a time you put your money in your purse and went to the market to buy a bag full of groceries. Now you take a bag of money, go to the market, and bring the groceries home in your purse."

Of course Reagan also had an anecdote to put a humorous slant on his frustration with the lack of support his plan received in certain circles:

"I often get weary of the great seers and prophets in the financial and political worlds, some optimistic, some pessimistic, who, even if they don't know how to predict accurately, at least know how to predict often.

"It reminds me of the sweet revenge that one businessman had recently when he told a company economist who was jumping out of the upper-story window, 'Don't worry, Herb, you'll be bottoming out soon.'"

~

Reagan often made the point that he was put in the position of cleaning up an economic mess left by his predecessors, as had another President before him:

"I feel a great affinity for James Madison. I'm told his worry over the size of the national debt drove him to distraction. I can sympathize; the debt was not of his making, either."

When he found a metaphor for balancing the budget, Reagan hit on the phrase his wife would pick up for her national campaign against drug abuse:

"Balancing the budget is a little like protecting your virtue: you just have to learn to say no."

Stopping tax hikes was crucial to the Reagan economic plan. In the same way he believed big government should get off people's backs, he believed that the hand of the tax collector should stay out of their pockets. He told Congress:

"We survived a Great Depression that toppled governments. We came back from Pearl Harbor to win the greatest military victory in world history.

"Today's living Americans have fought harder, paid a higher price for freedom, and done more to advance the dignity of man than any people who ever lived.

"We have in my lifetime gone from the horse and buggy to putting men on the moon and bringing them safely home.

"Now, don't tell us that we can't be trusted with a great share of our own earnings."

∼

Reagan wanted to set the record straight about how Medicare was going to be affected by his tax cuts and the reduction in government spending:

"In spite of all the stories you hear on television, the truth is that this administration will devote more money to health care than any other administration in history. It may come as a surprise, but forty-nine million elderly, poor, and disabled Americans will be served through Medicare and Medicaid in 1984. That's three million more than in 1980.

"With this kind of solid record, you can see why I get a little irritated with our critics. They remind me of the hypochondriac who was complaining to the doctor. He said, 'My left arm hurts me, also my left foot, and my back. Oh, and there's my hip and, oh, yes, my neck.'

"Well, the doctor muttered something to himself and then sat him down, crossed his legs, and tapped him with the little rubber hammer. Doc says, 'How are you now?' And he says, 'Now my knee hurts too.'"

∾

Reagan liked to poke fun at Speaker of the House Tip O'Neill, a Democrat who did not see eye-to-eye with Reagan's plan to limit taxation and government spending:

"There are some things that are current today and sweeping the country that I haven't had time to get familiar with — Pac-Man, for example. I asked about it and somebody told me that it was a round thing that gobbled up money. I thought that was Tip O'Neill."

∾

During his remarks and a question-and-answer session with reporters on the second anniversary of his inauguration, on January 20, 1983, President Reagan said:

"I see an American economy and an America on the mend."

∾

In describing Congress's habit of taxing and spending, Reagan put a twist on a favorite Will Rogers line:

"If I could paraphrase Will Rogers's line about never having met a man he didn't like, it seems government has never met a tax that it didn't hike."

Government

In the same way he believed Americans would stimulate the economy if they were given control over more of their income, Reagan believed Americans could solve many of their own problems better than a large, centralized federal government.

Reagan had this to say about government in his first inauguration speech:

"It is not my intention to do away with government. It is rather to make it work — work with us, not over us; stand by our side, not ride on our back. Government can and must provide opportunity, not smother it; foster productivity, not stifle it."

⁓

Naturally, Reagan had a story that summed up his sentiment about decentralizing government and giving the American people the freedom to solve their own problems:

"A hundred and fifty years ago the Frenchman Alexis de Tocqueville visited this country to find out the secret to our success. 'America is great because America is good,' he has been quoted as saying. 'And if America ever ceases to be good, America will cease to be great.' He gave examples of how someone in the community would see a problem, and he would talk to a few neighbors about it, and the next thing you knew, a committee was formed, and the people were solving the problem without any bureaucracy involved at all.

"We still do. And I like it that way."

⁓

Reagan quickly proved that he was committed to making changes to make the government work:

"When we came to Washington, we made quite a stir. Everybody found out that we were going to do just what we said we were going to do."

∾

Reagan thought it was about time people in Washington took responsibility for the problems they faced, rather than passing the buck:

"If we mean to continue governing [we] must realize that it will not always be so easy to place the blame on the past for our national difficulties. You know, one day the great baseball manager Frankie Frisch sent a rookie out to play center field. The rookie promptly dropped the first fly ball that was hit to him. On the next play he let a grounder go between his feet and then threw the ball to the wrong base. Frankie stormed out of the dugout, took his glove away from him, and said, 'I'll show you how to play the position.' And the next batter slammed a line drive right over second base. Frankie came in on it, missed it completely, fell down when he tried to chase it, threw down his glove, and yelled at the rookie, 'You've got center field so screwed up nobody can play it.'"

∾

Reagan liked to joke about the absurdity of some government regulations:

"A city had decided it was going to raise its traffic signs. They were five feet high, and they were going to raise them to seven. The federal government stepped in and volunteered with a program to do it. They came in and lowered the streets two feet."

∾

Reagan understood that downsizing was not the natural instinct:

"No government ever voluntarily reduces itself in size. Government programs, once launched, never disappear. Actually, a government bureau is the nearest thing to eternal life we'll ever see on this earth."

~

In his address to the New York City Partnership Association on January 14, 1982:

"Government is the people's business, and every man, woman, and child becomes a shareholder with the first penny of tax paid."

~

Toward the end of his first term, Reagan was proud of the progress he had made in reducing the size of the federal government:

"I almost forgot something else you and I can feel mighty good about. Americans will spend three hundred million fewer hours on government paperwork this year than they were doing when we took office. The bureaucratic monster who would slay private enterprise is learning a new command, and it's called 'Heel.'"

~

During a question-and-answer with the press on January 20, 1983, when asked a question regarding political philosophy, Reagan quipped:

"The question was, am I concerned about being identified as looking too much like a moderate. I have to say, you must be doing something right when you're getting rocks thrown at you from both sides."

~

In his remarks and a question-and-answer session with members of the Massachusetts High Technology Council in Bedford on January 26, 1983, Reagan said:

"I've had the privilege of looking into America's future today, and the future looks good. And I know that you're aware I've given a bedrock speech or two about the principles that we must get back to in our country — reducing tax rates, the growth of federal spending, reviving the magic of the market, and bringing government closer to the people. The trouble is, sometimes those principles seem about as popular in Washington as mandating a fourteen-hour workday on Christmas."

Communism

Reagan felt it was of vital importance to contain communism. He saw that form of totalitarianism as the greatest threat to individual freedom and democracy in the world.

"You know, there are only two places where communism works: in heaven, where they don't need it, and in hell, where they've already got it."

~

During his speech to Britain's Parliament in 1982:

"It is the Soviet Union that runs against the tide of history. . . . [It is] the march of freedom and democracy which will leave Marxism-Leninism on the ash heap of history as it has left other tyrannies which stifle the freedom and muzzle the self-expression of the people."

~

In his remarks at the centennial meeting of the Supreme Council of the Knights of Columbus in Hartford, Connecticut, on August 3, 1982, Reagan said:

"Now, I must say, my remarks on this occasion have not drawn rave reviews from the Soviet press. In fact, *Pravda* suggested that my remarks were hysterical and the work of an intellectual pygmy. And a Polish newspaper under martial law there called it a cesspool of invectives, insults, and insinuation. Well, now, naturally, as a former actor, I'm somewhat sensitive about how the press notices that."

~

Speech to the National Association of Evangelicals, March 8, 1983:

"Let us beware that while they [Soviet rulers] preach the supremacy of the state, declare its omnipotence over individual man, and predict its eventual domination over all the peoples of the earth, they are the focus of evil in the modern world. . . . I urge you to beware the temptation . . . to ignore the facts of history and the aggressive impulses of any evil empire, to simply call the arms race a giant misunderstanding and thereby remove yourself from the struggle between right and wrong, good and evil."

~

"Yes, let us pray for the salvation of all of those who live in that totalitarian darkness — pray they will discover the joy of knowing God. But until they do, let us be aware that while they preach the supremacy of the state, declare its omnipotence over individual man, and predict its eventual domination of all peoples on the earth, they are the focus of evil in the modern world."

∽

"Did you hear that the communists now have a million-dollar lottery for their people? The winners get a dollar a year for a million years."

Defense

Reagan made defense an issue in the 1980 campaign. He believed that a strong military defense was essential if the United States were to remain a superpower. Reagan believed that in order for the United States to negotiate arms reductions with the Soviet Union, the United States had to be negotiating as a powerhouse, not as a weak team begging the other guys for favors.

Despite his efforts to cut government spending, Reagan also thought it was vital for the United States to maintain strong defenses:

"To those who say that we can't cut spending, lower tax rates, reduce inflation, and, yes, rebuild defenses we need in this dangerous world, I have a six-word answer: Yes, we can, yes, we must!"

∽

"Our military strength is a prerequisite to peace, but let it be clear we maintain this strength in the hope it will never be used, for the ultimate determinant in the struggle that's going on in the world will not be bombs and rockets, but a test of wills and ideas, a trial of spiritual resolve, the values we hold, the beliefs we cherish, the ideals to which we are dedicated."

~

"We're a nation with global responsibilities. We're not somewhere else in the world protecting someone else's interests; we're there protecting our own."

~

"The most fundamental paradox is that if we're never to use force, we must be prepared to use it and to use it successfully. We Americans don't want war and we don't start fights. We don't maintain a strong military force to conquer or coerce others. The purpose of our military is simple and straightforward: we want to prevent war by deterring others from the aggression that caused war. If our efforts are successful, we will have peace and never be forced into battle. There will never be a need to fire a single shot. That's the paradox of deterrence."

~

"Some even argue that if we really wanted to reduce nuclear weapons, we should simply stop building them ourselves. That argument makes about as much sense as saying that the way to prevent fires is to close down the fire department."

~

"Peace is an objective, not a policy."

~

"Let me share with you a vision of the future which offers hope. It is that we embark on a program to counter the awesome Soviet military threat with measures that are defensive. Let us turn to the very strengths in technology that spawned our great industrial base and that have given us the quality of life we enjoy today."

~

In the introduction of his remarks on signing the Nuclear Waste Policy Act of 1982 on January 7, 1983, Reagan said:

"You must know that something good has happened when you see all these members of the Congress and of the administration and we're all smiling at the same time."

~

"I remember the first time I visited a nuclear power facility.

"In one building they were showing me through, we put on felt boots and gowns and we went through.

"Afterward, we had to peel all of it off. And there was a slot machine there in which you put your hands and your feet — and there were four dials that started ticking away measuring the amount of radioactivity that you might have picked up in your extremities.

"The dials were all fine, except on my left hand. The dial kept on ticking, and it was getting up to where the numbers were red. So I was getting a little concerned. The manager of the plant looked over my shoulder and said, "Oh, your left hand. That always happens. That's the radium dial on your wristwatch."

"I was very relieved. I was two hundred miles from there when I realized I don't have a radium dial.

"Every once in a while I still put my head under the covers and look to see if my hand is lighting up."

~

Mr. Reagan, still on the subject of nuclear power, joked about two farmers talking:

"One of them said to the other, 'Where would you like to be in the event of a nuclear explosion?' And the old boy said, 'Someplace where I could say, "What was that?"'"

During the 1984 presidential campaign, Reagan said this:

"And I just happen to believe that we cannot go into another generation with the world living under the threat of those weapons and knowing that some madman can push the button someplace. It doesn't even have to be one of the superpowers. A war could probably be triggered, as nuclear weapons proliferate, by someone else doing it."

Milestones

As in each presidency, Reagan's first four years were marked by a number of triumphs and tragedies.

On October 23, 1983, 241 U.S. marines and sailors were killed by a suicide bomber in a terrorist attack on their barracks in Beirut, Lebanon. Reagan wanted those held responsible to be dealt with by a firm hand:

"The Beirut bombing is a terrible example of what is one of my most frustrating and greatest concerns — the increased use of government-backed terror. . . .

"The civilized nations have to end this assult on humanity, but not in blind revenge. I've never believed we have a right to slaughter innocent civilians in the hope we'll get some of the guilty."

∼

Two days later, on October 25, 1983, U.S. marines and rangers with a force from the Caribbean nations invaded the island of Grenada. A week before, Marxist prime minister Maurice Bishop had been executed by a more leftist rebel group. The Caribbean nations asked the U.S. to help them restore order:

"The hardest decision for a President to make is the one that must order our young servicemen to go someplace where their lives will be endangered. Regrettably, there were some deaths during the Grenada landing. But I was proud of all those young men in uniform."

∼

Some people questioned the President's judgment when he invaded Grenada, an island most Americans had never heard of until the military action was reported in the news. However, as the President pointed out, all was not as it appeared to be:

"Grenada, we were told, was a friendly island paradise for tourism. Well, it wasn't. It was a Soviet-Cuban colony, being readied as a major bastion to export terror and undermine democracy. We got there just in time."

❧

Reagan, speaking to supporters a few weeks after the American liberation of the island of Grenada from communist aggressors:

"I received a copy of a story written by one of our air force pilots for the *Armed Forces Journal.* He recounted as how he noticed that every news story about the Grenada rescue mission contained a line that Grenada produces more nutmeg than any other place in the world. He decided that was a code, and that he was going to break the code — and he did:

"Number one, Grenada produces more nutmeg than any place in the world. Number two, the Soviets and the Cubans are trying to take Grenada. Number three, you can't make good eggnog without nutmeg. Number four, you can't have Christmas without eggnog. Number five, the Soviets and the Cubans are trying to steal Christmas. And number six, we stopped them."

❧

After visiting with the families of the deceased, Reagan had to face the rest of his schedule. He wrote in his diary that night:

"Nancy and I met individually all the families of the deceased. We were both in tears. All I could do was grip her hands. I was too choked up to speak. . . . [Later] home to change clothes and off to the White House correspondents dinner. I was supposed to do a routine of jokes, etc. I couldn't change gears that swiftly. So as not to put a damper on the evening . . . I waited till the last and then asked their pardon for not 'singing for my supper' because of our sad journey to Andrews Air Force Base."

∾

Reagan went to Normandy, France, on June 6, 1984, to take part in a celebration commemorating the fortieth anniversary of D-Day. At this ceremony Reagan said:

"We will always remember. We will always be proud. We will always be prepared, so we may always be free."

∾

Later in the same speech he said:

"Forty summers have passed since the battle that you fought here. You were young the day you took these cliffs; some of you were hardly more than boys, with the deepest joys of life before you. Yet you risked everything here. Why? Why did you do it? What impelled you to put aside the instinct for self-preservation and risk your lives to take these cliffs? What inspired all the men of the armies that met here? We look at you, and somehow we know the answer. It was faith and belief; it was loyalty and love.

"You all knew that some things are worth dying for. One's country is worth dying for, and democracy is worth dying for, because it's the most deeply honorable form of government ever devised by man. All of you loved liberty. All of you were willing to fight tyranny, and you knew the people of your countries were behind you."

∾

On the same European tour, Reagan stopped in Ballyporeen, Ireland, which gave him an opportunity to reflect on his own ancestral routes:

"So this was home. This was where my people came from in ages past. That's the great thing about America, we all come from someplace else. We all have roots that reach somewhere far away. Even the Native American Indian apparently came across from Asia when there was a land bridge leading to North America tens of thousands of years ago. We all have another home."

Humor and the Press

Just before his first term, Reagan said, "I think there is historically an adversary relationship between the government and the press, and I think it's proper. But I think it is overdone at times and can be just for the purpose of being an adversary." During his eight years in the White House, Reagan was surrounded by reporters and photographers and often poked fun to lighten up a relationship that was tense just by its very nature.

While some leaks are hardly a laughing matter, Reagan often joked about leaks in general:

"Official Washington's fascination with passing trends and one-day headlines can sometimes cause serious problems — like leaks. Before we even announced the giveaway of surplus cheese, the warehouse mice had hired a lobbyist."

~

When asked what he thought was responsible for his continued popularity with the American people, Reagan said:

"I don't really know . . . unless maybe — maybe the people have a way of sensing that I like them. And I do. I don't know how anyone could be in this business and not like people."

During National Volunteer Week:

"I realize there's a theory that good news is not good for the ratings, but I would like to suggest to the media that during National Volunteer Week they give attention to America's heroic private-sector initiatives. Then, if the ratings go down, they can go back to the bad news."

~

Reagan was asked by a *People* magazine reporter if his bulletproof shirt or jacket hung in the family quarters or whether the Secret Service kept it someplace else:

Reagan: "No, no. They keep it. And they come with it in hand, and they kind of come in flinching because they know I don't accept it with good grace."
Reporter: "What do you say when they put it on you?"
Reagan: "Oh, even an occasional unprintable word."
Reporter: "Is it bulky or heavy?"
Reagan: "Well, it's bulky. And I work so hard in the gym. Everybody will think I'm getting fat."

~

During his remarks at the annual dinner of the White House Correspondents' Association on April 13, 1984, Reagan said:

"Well, I know this: I've laid down the law, though, to everyone from now on about anything that happens, that no matter what time it is, wake me, even if it's in the middle of a cabinet meeting."

◦

During a question-and-answer with the press on January 11, 1983, Reagan thought he'd try to straighten out the problem of "leaks" versus facts reported by the press:

Reporter: "Have you really had leaks up to your keister, sir?"
The President: "I didn't expect that to be quoted."
Reporter: "How is your keister, sir?"
The President: "I'd like to go back to those days when the press voluntarily never quoted a President without his permission. You have permission to quote me."
Reporter: "Thank you."

◦

Reagan, speaking to a group of crusty old newspaper reporters, tried to illustrate how hard they are to impress:

"You know, in the old days of vaudeville, it used to be that ambitious young vaudevillians would go into an old empty theater and try out in front of a blasé booking agent who'd be sitting there in one of the front seats with a cigar, all alone in the theater, watching them do their act — and he was very hard to please.

"One young fellow walked out to center stage. The agent asked him what he did, and the kid just took off and flew around the whole theater — made a couple of circles clear up to the ceiling, came back down, and landed back at the center of the stage.

"The agent says, 'What else do you do besides bird imitations?'"

~

During a question-and-answer session on March 4, 1983, a reporter announced, "Mr. President, unfortunately our time is nearly up, so this will be our last question." Laughter followed Reagan's sarcastic response of, "Oh, dear."

~

Reagan responded to an introduction given by Clare Boothe Luce, in which she read some gloomy passages from the memoirs of former Presidents about the burden. After Ms. Luce dramatized the heavy burdens and personal sacrifices it takes to be President, Reagan responded: "Well . . . , Clare, I must be doing something wrong. I'm kind of enjoying myself."

~

To the members of the press at the annual Gridiron Dinner on April 23, 1985:

"We're all Americans together and we believe in the same ideals. It's good to be here and for you folks on the beat tomorrow, sleep late. I'm going to."

~

During an informal exchange with reporters on August 22, 1983:

Reporter: "How is your hearing?"
The President: "What?"

∾

After the U.S. Navy shot down two Libyan jets over the Gulf of Sidra, Reagan addressed a story played up by the press:

"And there's been a lot of talk, and the press has been very concerned, because six hours went by before they awoke me at four-thirty in the morning to tell me about it. And there's a very good answer to that. Why? If our planes were shot down, yes, they'd wake me up right away; if other fellows were shot down, why wake me?"

∾

During an informal exchange with reporters on April 7, 1983:

Reporter: "What are you going to tell the Chinese ambassador?"
The President: "Hello."

∾

Reagan told reporters at the White House Correspondents' Association Dinner in 1985:

"It's my job to solve all the country's problems, and it's your job to make sure no one finds out about it."

∾

At the annual awards dinner of the White House News Photographers' Association on May 27, 1987, Reagan remarked about Sam Donaldson:

"Somebody asked me one day why we didn't put a stop to Sam's shouting out questions at us when we're out on the South Lawn. We can't. If we did, the starlings would come back."

~

In his remarks at the annual dinner of the White House Correspondents' Association on April 13, 1984:

"I heard Lesley Stahl [CBS News] has been asking if anything can be done to improve my answers. Yes, ask better questions."

~

At the annual Gridiron Dinner on April 28, 1987:

"Incidentally, I've got a news item for you: We have a spin-off from our Star Wars research. It's a helmet for me to wear at press conferences. All I do is push a button and it shoots down incoming questions."

~

Remarks by telephone to the annual dinner of the White House Correspondents' Association on April 25, 1981:

"Well, I'm looking forward to the next news conference. I have so many questions to ask you all."

~

At the annual dinner of the White House Correspondents' Association on April 13, 1984:

"Nancy's taken to watching the press conferences, and now every time I answer a question, she says, 'I have a follow-up.'"

∾

After reports that the President always first pointed at female reporters dressed in red during questions at his press conferences, Reagan said at the annual dinner of the White House Correspondents' Association on April 17, 1986:

"At my last press conference, I thought that gimmick of wearing a red dress to get my attention went a little too far, but it was a nice try, Sam."

∾

On a more serious note, Reagan had a definite opinion about the press and the ethics of its reporting:

"As I have said before, a free and aggressive press corps is essential to the health of our democracy. If the press does not tell us, who will? But with that freedom comes a special responsibility to be accurate and fair. The press should remember the great impact its words can have on a person's life. Sadly, the words *questioned about* sometimes translate into *guilty of* in the minds of readers and listeners. That does not mean that reporters shouldn't do their job. It just means they should be careful."

∾

"Mike Deaver said I have a short attention span," he said. "I was going to reply to that, but what the hell, let's move on to something else."

~

"Every President will try to use the press to his best advantage. But the press is not a weak sister that needs bracing. The press can take care of itself and a President should be able to take care of himself as well."

~

During remarks and a question-and-answer session with reporters on strategic arms reduction and military deterrence on January 14, 1983, a reporter misspoke:

Reporter: "Mr. Secretary — Mr. President, excuse me —"
Other Reporter: "Who?"
Reporter: "Mr. President —"
The President: "Gee, I thought for a minute I'd lost my job."

~

In a question-and-answer session with network anchors on the State of the Union address on January 25, 1983, Reagan told reporters:

"I'm supposed to get out of here in like two and a half minutes and not interrupt any of the other briefings that you've had. I really came in to tell all of you that everything you've heard is off the record."

~

During his remarks at a Republican Party rally in Cape Girardeau, Missouri, on September 14, 1988, Reagan quoted a political commentator,

Mark Heplin, to back up a point he was making about the economy. After quoting the journalist, Reagan said:

"I'll bet a lot of the press didn't think I'd ever be quoting one of them."

~

The *Chicago Tribune* reported on April 23, 1987, that President Reagan poked some fun at journalists but ended his speech at the White House Correspondents' Association annual dinner with a plea for peace with the media. After taking the potshots, Reagan confessed, "I have a positive opinion of reporters."

~

The Associated Press reported on April 22, 1988, that Reagan joked about books that would be written by ex-aides and about his "own mental faculties" during his seventh and last appearance at the White House Correspondents' Association Dinner:

"What I hope my epitaph will be with the White House correspondents, what every President's epitaph should be, is 'He gave as good as he got.' That, I think, makes for a healthy press and a healthy presidency."

To the Photographers

In his remarks at the annual awards dinner of the White House News Photographers' Association on May 18, 1983, Reagan quipped:

"I'm told that there's a feeling among photographers that journalists don't treat you well or as fairly as you'd like. Welcome to the club."

~

"You know, I like your White House photographers' motto, 'One picture is worth a thousand denials.'"

~

"There are some things that you and I have in common in addition to being on opposite ends of the camera. For you, the darkroom is a place to develop film. For me, it's a place Democrats use as a think tank."

~

"Just the other day, I saw my first robin red breast of the spring in a tree outside the Oval Office — and six of you in the bushes."

~

Reagan went to a White House News Photographers' Association dinner expecting to see the press corps in its usual casual wear, appropriate for chasing down a good shot.

"I want to tell you, though, I had a bad moment — or Nancy and I did when we came in here. You're all so beautifully dressed and dressed up that we thought maybe we'd gotten to the wrong dinner."

~

"But on the level, though, I like photographers. You don't ask questions."

~

Reagan had a newspaper story of his own to tell:

"A newspaper photographer was called by his editor and told of a raging fire. The photographer's assignment was to rush down to the local airport, board a waiting plane, go out and get some pictures of the fire, and be back in time for the afternoon edition.

"Well, he raced down the freeway, broke all the traffic laws, got to the airport, drove his car to the end of the runway, and sure enough, there was a plane revving up its engines, ready to go.

"He jumped in the plane shouting, 'Let's go!' and they were off. At about five thousand feet he began getting his camera out of the bag and told the fellow flying the plane to get him over the fire so he could get his pictures and get back to the paper.

"From the other side of the cockpit there was a deafening silence, and then he heard the words he will always remember: 'Aren't you the instructor?'"

∽

"There isn't a person here who isn't willing to go to great lengths to get a good shot. Just this afternoon I stepped outside the Oval Office to feed the squirrels. Six photographers came out of the bushes. It's okay. I had enough peanuts to go around."

∽

"It's not easy having so many photographers around," he said. "For instance, I told everybody — my right side is my good side. My far right side. Keeping my right side to the cameras is no problem when I walk home from the Oval Office in the evening. Morning's a different thing.

You know what it's like to start the day by walking to the office backwards?"

∼

In 1984 Reagan was unchallenged by anyone in his own party, but seven Democrats ran against each other in the primaries. Reagan said this at the annual dinner of the White House News Photographers' Association:

"I know this isn't a partisan political affair. But I also know that you have wide-angle lenses that are wide enough to get all the Democratic presidential candidates in one shot. You just don't have a lens that's wide enough to get all their promises . . ."

∼

Reagan was attending the annual dinner of the White House News Photographers' Association. It was a chance for the President and the photographers to poke fun, away from the demands of the job:

"Now I've been told that this is all off the record and that the cameras are all off. Is that right? Because I've been waiting years to do this . . ."

At this point, the President jammed his thumbs in his ears and wiggled his fingers at the audience.

Second Term

Reagan continued his policy to improve the economy and downsize the federal government. He also stepped up efforts to forge a working relationship with Gorbachev in order to negotiate nuclear-warhead limits with the Soviet Union. These efforts resulted in four historic summits with the Soviet Union.

Just before his second inauguration a reporter asked Reagan, "In your own mind, what's the most important thing for you to do between now and 1988?"

Reagan answered, "Get us back on a solid economy and get us to the point that if we haven't by then been able to eliminate the deficit spending, at least we could see a definite date at which it would be eliminated and then set in motion a program for reducing the national debt. On the international scene, to continue on a program for peace — and the goal is the ultimate elimination of nuclear weapons."

Reagan didn't have to worry about adjusting to the busy presidential schedule at the beginning of his second term. He had also learned in his first four years that the satisfaction he got from his job stemmed from the connection it gave him with other human beings:

"One of the unexpected pleasures of the presidency has nothing to do with economic problems or international crisis. It is the opportunity to lend a hand now and then to other human beings."

Milestones

Remarks at Bitburg Air Force Base, Federal Republic of Germany, on May 5, 1985:

"Twenty-two years ago President John F. Kennedy went to the Berlin Wall and proclaimed that he, too, was a Berliner. I am a Berliner. I am an

Afghan, and I am a prisoner of the gulag. I am a refugee in a crowded boat foundering off the coast of Vietnam. I am a Laotian, a Cambodian, a Cuban, and a Miskito Indian."

Remarks on the *Challenger* shuttle disaster delivered at the Oval Office on January 28, 1986:

"Nineteen years ago, almost to the day, we lost three astronauts in a terrible accident on the ground. But we've never lost an astronaut in flight; we've never had a tragedy like this. And perhaps we've forgotten the courage it took for the crew of the shuttle; but they, the *Challenger* Seven, were aware of the dangers, but overcame them and did their jobs brilliantly. We mourn seven heroes: Michael Smith, Dick [Francis] Scobee, Judith Resnik, Ronald McNair, Ellison Onizuka, Gregory Jarvis, and Christa McAuliffe. We mourn their loss as a nation together.

"For the families of the seven, we cannot bear, as you do, the full impact of this tragedy. But we feel the loss, and we're thinking about you so very much. Your loved ones were daring and brave, and they had that special grace, that special spirit that says, 'Give me a challenge and I'll meet it with joy.' They had a hunger to explore the universe and discover its truths. They wished to serve, and they did. They served all of us.

"We've grown used to wonders in this century. It's hard to dazzle us. But for twenty-five years the United States space program has been doing just that. We've grown used to the idea of space, and perhaps we forget that we've only just begun. We're still pioneers. They, the members of the *Challenger* crew, were pioneers.

"And I want to say something to the schoolchildren of America who were watching the live coverage of the shuttle's takeoff. I know it is hard to understand, but sometimes painful things like this happen. It's all part of the process of exploration and discovery. It's all a part of taking a chance and expanding man's horizons. The future doesn't belong to the faint-hearted; it belongs to the brave. The *Challenger* crew was pulling us into the future, and we'll continue to follow them. . . .

"There's a coincidence today. On this day 390 years ago, the great explorer Sir Francis Drake died aboard ship off the coast of Panama. In his lifetime the great frontiers were the oceans, and a historian later said, 'He lived by the sea, died on it, and was buried in it.' Well, today we can say of the *Challenger* crew: Their direction was, like Drake's, complete.

"The crew of the space shuttle *Challenger* honored us by the manner in which they lived their lives. We will never forget them, nor the last time we saw them, this morning, as they prepared for the journey and waved good-bye and 'slipped the surly bonds of Earth to touch the face of God.'"

∾

Reflecting on the life of Martin Luther King, Jr., Reagan said:

"I didn't appreciate what a remarkable man he was while he was living. But I suppose that's the way it is with prophets. You sometimes don't know their impact and importance until they're gone."

∾

On April 14, 1986, American war planes bombed "terrorist-related" targets in Libya. The U.S. action was in retaliation for the Libyan bombing of a discotheque in West Berlin that caused the death of an American serviceman. It was also hoped that a show of American force would deter future terrorists' attacks:

"We Americans are slow to anger. We always seek peaceful avenues before resorting to the use of force — and we did. We tried quiet diplomacy, public condemnation, economic sanctions, and demonstrations of military force. None succeeded. Despite our repeated warnings, Qaddafi continued his reckless policy of terror. He counted on America to be passive. He counted wrong."

~

On July 3, 1986, Reagan delivered his remarks at the Statue of Liberty Centennial ceremonies:

"Our helicopter would circle around the top of the statue. I was carried away. She was so feminine, which I never realized before. I told Nancy, 'This is the other woman in my life.'"

~

During his European tour in the summer of 1987, Reagan faced perhaps one of his biggest moral dilemmas when he had to decide whether or not to visit a cemetery in Bitburg, West Germany, where two thousand German war dead were buried:

"What we didn't know was that forty-eight members of the Nazi SS were also buried there. . . . I made the decision, however, that we must go. I didn't feel that we could ask new generations of Germans to live with this guilt forever without any hope of redemption. They were not alive during World War Two. These young people should not be made to bear the burden."

Government

Reagan continued pressing for a smaller federal government. He also continued ribbing opponents and joking with the press and the American people about the progress his administration had made. After all, as he said himself, "At my age I didn't go to Washington to play politics as usual."

"The big spenders in Washington would have been right at home with Oscar Wilde. He's the one who said that he knew of only one way to get rid of temptation: 'Yield to it.'"

~

In his remarks to the White House Conference on Small Business, August 15, 1986:

"Government's view of the economy could be summed up in a few short phrases: If it moves, tax it. If it keeps moving, regulate it. And if it stops moving, subsidize it."

~

"Our opponents try to cure fever by eating the thermometer."

~

In his remarks at a Human Rights Day event, December 10, 1986:

"The other day, someone told me the difference between a democracy and a people's democracy. It's the same difference between a jacket and a straightjacket."

~

This was a story Reagan liked to tell to illustrate how his administration was eliminating bureaucratic red tape:

"Jerry Carmen, a commonsense, independent businessman from New Hampshire, heads up the General Services Administration for me.

"He told journalist Don Lambro about a warehouse with a leaky roof that he went to inspect one Saturday, early in his tenure at GSA. Arriving back at his office, he said, 'I asked the people in charge, wasn't that a pretty poor warehouse? And they agreed it was. Well then, I asked them, shouldn't it be closed? And they all said yes. I asked, why don't we? Well, they said, we're going to do a study first. The study was going to cost five hundred thousand dollars. I said, do I have the power to close it? They said that I did. And I did.'"

~

During an appearance at a food bank's warehouse facility, Reagan said:

"We just used to call it neighborliness in our country, until the government started sticking its nose in. Well, if you want to put the government's nose out of shape, I won't be mad."

~

In his State of the Union address on February 4, 1986, Reagan said:

"Government growing beyond our consent had become a lumbering giant, slamming shut the gates of opportunity, threatening to crush the very roots of our freedom. What brought America back? The American people brought us back — with quiet courage and common sense; with undying faith that in this nation under God the future will be ours, for the future belongs to the free."

~

One thing Reagan always took seriously was the tradition of individualism in this country, and fighting the government programs that threatened it:

"If we're to renew America, we must stop trying to homogenize it."

~

Mr. Reagan, signing the government Prompt Payment Act, which had been delayed a day:

"I would have signed it right away except the government didn't pay its pen bill on time, so I didn't have anything to write with."

~

Mr. Reagan was asked what advice he would give to a young person going out in the world today:

"Vote Republican."

~

Reagan believed that not only should the American people have their tax burden lightened, but that the tax system should be something every taxpayer could understand:

"Our tax system should be made more simple, fair, and rewarding for the people. Would you believe that even Albert Einstein had to ask the IRS for help on his 1040?"

~

And, of course, the activities of the government reminded Reagan of an old tale he knew:

"Sometimes government programs remind me of the country preacher who called on a town one hundred miles from his own. He went there for the revival meeting.

"Going to church, he noticed a man seated on the porch of a little country store who was from his hometown, a fellow who was known for his drinking.

"The minister went up to him and asked him what he was doing so far from home. 'Preacher,' he said, 'beer is five cents a bottle cheaper here.'

"The minister told him that it didn't make much sense, what with the expense of traveling all that way and back, and the price of lodging and whatnot.

"The drinker thought for a moment and then replied, 'Preacher, I'm not stupid. I just sit here until I show a profit.'"

~

Reagan wanted the state and federal governments to find a way to work together and have more faith in each other. He used this fishing story to describe the state of that relationship:

"Two partners decided to take the day off and go fishing. They'd rowed out into the middle of the lake, baited the hooks, and were waiting for the first bite when all of a sudden one of them said, 'Sam, oh my gosh! We forgot to close the safe.' 'So what,' said Sam, 'we're both here, aren't we?'

"For too long that's the kind of partnership the federal government and the states have had. Neither really trusted the other, but Washington has been dipping into the cash drawer when the states weren't looking."

The Abortion Issue

Abortion was an issue during Reagan's first term, but it moved to the forefront of the political arena during his second term. To Reagan, it was never a political issue, but rather a question of morality. Throughout the debate his view never wavered:

"Until someone can prove the unborn child is not a life, shouldn't we give it the benefit of the doubt and assume it is?"

~

Reagan said this of the lives lost to abortion:

"These children, over tenfold the number of Americans lost in all our nation's wars, will never laugh, never sing, never experience the joy of human love; nor will they strive to heal the sick, or feed the poor, or make peace among nations. Abortion has denied them the first and most basic of human rights, and we are infinitely poorer for their loss."

Foreign Affairs and Defense

Mr. Reagan, meeting with the Los Angeles Raiders following their 1984 Super Bowl Championship:

"Congratulations, Coach Flores, but you've caused me some problems. I've already received a call from Moscow. They think that Marcus Allen is a new secret weapon, and they insist that we dismantle it.

"But seriously, you've given me an idea. If you'd turn your team over to us, we'd put them in silos and we wouldn't have to build the MX missile."

❧

During his remarks and a question-and-answer session with members of the Commonwealth Club of California in San Francisco on March 4, 1983, Reagan said:

"We and our trading partners are in the same boat. If one partner shoots a hole in the bottom of the boat, does it make sense for the other partner to shoot another hole in the boat? There are those who say yes, and call it getting tough. I call it getting wet — all over."

❧

Later, during an address to the General Assembly of the United Nations, on September 21, 1987, President Reagan said:

"In our obsession with antagonisms of the moment, we often forget how much unites all the members of humanity. Perhaps we need some outside, universal threat to recognize this common bond. I occasionally think how quickly our differences would vanish if we were facing an alien threat from outside this world."

❧

Eastern Europe went through changes during the Reagan presidency that were unthinkable even ten years earlier. The President applauded each time an oppressive regime was torn down and tried to foster trade relations that would benefit both countries whenever possible.

"Poland is not East or West. Poland is at the center of European civilization. It has contributed mightily to that civilization. It is doing so today by being magnificently unreconciled to oppression."

~

"I want to state emphatically that if the outrages in Poland do not cease, we cannot and will not conduct 'business as usual' with the perpetrators who aid and abet them. Make no mistake, their crime will cost them dearly in future dealings with America and free peoples everywhere. I do not make this statement lightly, or without serious reflection."

~

Reagan found a kindred spirit in former British prime minister Margaret Thatcher. He often called her "the other woman in my life."

~

When Reagan visited West Berlin in 1987, he sent a message over the Berlin Wall:

"To those listening in East Berlin, a special word: Although I cannot be with you, I address my remarks to you just as surely as to those standing here before me. For I join you, as I join your fellow countrymen in the West, in this firm, this unalterable belief: *Es gibt nur ein Berlin.*" ["There is only one Berlin."]

~

Central America was another place of concern. Reagan dedicated a lot of his personal energy to getting Congress to appropriate military and financial support to fighting the Communist forces there:

"Why are we concerned about El Salvador? For one, it is closer to Texas than Texas is to Massachusetts.

"Now, I mean geographically, not necessarily ideologically."

∼

"The national security of all the Americas is at state in Central America. If we cannot defend ourselves there, we cannot expect to prevail elsewhere. Our credibility would collapse, our alliances would crumble, and the safety of our homeland would be put in jeopardy. We have a vital interest, a moral duty, and a solemn responsibility."

∼

In 1983 Reagan said this, comparing the Soviet influence in Libya to that in Central America.

"The Soviet [Union] is a hostile influence there . . . just as the Soviet Union is involved in what is going on in Central America. It is time that more people in the world and certainly in our country realize the Soviet Union is bent on imperialism, on expansion and aggression. Where there is trouble, they love to stir the pot, and this they're doing."

∼

Remarks at the Conservative Political Action Conference in Washington, D.C., on March 1, 1985:

"I've spoken recently of the freedom fighters, and we owe them our help. . . . They are the moral equal of our Founding Fathers and the brave men and women of the French Resistance. We cannot turn away from them, for the struggle here is not right versus left; it is right versus wrong."

Iran-Contra

The Iran-Contra affair was, in the end, a black mark on the Reagan presidency. Although the President himself was never implicated, it caused many to question his method of delegating authority. [In the mid-1980s, the CIA provided aid to the Contras, Nicaraguan rebels who were attempting to overthrow the Sandinista government. This aid was specifically forbidden by Congress.]

The *St. Petersburg Times* reported on March 18, 1988, that although a former national security adviser, Robert McFarlane, had pleaded guilty to four counts of withholding information from Congress, Mr. Reagan still claimed to know of no laws that were broken in the Iran-Contra affair. Reagan said:

"He just pleaded guilty to not telling Congress everything it wanted to know. I've done that myself," the President said. Catching himself, he quickly added, "Now don't distort that. . . . I just think Congress would like to be asking questions about almost anything."

~

For a long time it was not clear what the President did and did not know as the transactions were taking place. He finally clarified that in a public statement:

"A few months ago, I told the American people that I did not trade arms for hostages. My heart and my best intentions still tell me that's true, but the facts and the evidence tell me it is not. . . . Now, what should happen when you make a mistake is this: you take your knocks, you learn your lessons, and then you move on."

∾

In 1987 Reagan had this to say in an interview about the Iran-Contra affair:

"The reason we had to have a covert operation was we believed that the people who wanted to talk to us, their lives would be forfeited if the Ayatollah ever found out they were doing this. Through a third country which vouched for them, these individuals said we believe that shortly there's going to be a new government. . . . They then made the proposal; when we agreed and sent people to see them, they then raised an issue, would we provide them with some weapons. It was almost a token, the number of weapons that were to be provided. And they justified their claim on the basis that . . . this would give them some standing and prestige with the military and whoever was going to succeed [Ayatollah Khomeini]. . . . Now, I did not see this as trading arms for hostages in the way in which it was done. I was not doing anything for the kidnappers. I figured that if these people had any influence in their positions in Iran — well, they did. They got two freed, and we were told that two more were coming out within forty-eight hours at the time that the whole story broke open that this operation was going on. Now, we've had months and months of investigations about this, the extra money and where did it go. I am still waiting. I am the one who told the public and press that we, once this thing was revealed, had discovered that there had been extra money for the shipment of the arms. We've gotten the cost of the arms — $12.3 million — that's all there were. To this day, after all the investigations, I'm still waiting for an answer. Who raised the price to these individuals for the arms, who got the extra money, and where did the extra money go? All of the investigation had not revealed that. When I went public, that's what I said I needed to learn, that's why I appointed a commission of my own. And I couldn't find this out."

~

In a speech to the nation in August, Reagan apologized for the Iran-Contra scandal, saying, "The fact of the matter is that there's nothing I can say that will make the situation right." And he went on to say later in the same speech, "I was stubborn in my pursuit of a policy that went astray."

The Soviet Summits

Many consider the summits the crowning achievement of Reagan's second term. While the arms reduction negotiations did not always progress, there is no denying that the four meetings between Reagan and Gorbachev between 1986 and 1988 paved the way for a new relationship between the United States and what was then the Soviet Union.

Reagan described his Soviet counterpart this way:

"He is himself — no imitation of anyone that I've ever known. I found him quite different from other leaders of his country that I've spoken to. He had the stature that goes with his position. He really doesn't hold back. You don't get any feeling of cunning. He's straightforward. Margaret

Thatcher, one of the first Western leaders to meet with him, described him best when she said he's someone you 'can do business with.'"

~

"My hope is that the U.S.–Soviet relationship will continue on the path we have set for it. Our goal has been a stable, sustainable relationship, built on a realistic evaluation of our interests and Soviet policies and pursued through a candid dialogue."

~

In Reagan's *An American Life,* he wrote about his meetings with Gorbachev:

"We sat down beside the blazing hearth, just the two of us and our interpreters, and I told Gorbachev that I thought he and I were in a unique situation at a unique time: 'Here you and I are, two men in a room, probably the only two men in the world who could bring about World War Three. But by the same token, we may be the only two men in the world who could perhaps bring about peace in the world.'"

~

"I think our honesty helped the Soviets face up to their own weaknesses and uncertain future."

~

At a speech before the World Affairs Council:

"You know, in the Soviet Union, for a private citizen to buy an automobile, there is a ten-year waiting period. . . . You have to put the money down too, ten years in advance. So this man has gone in and he's doing all the signing, all the papers, and putting out his money. And finally, when he makes that final signature, the man behind the counter said, 'Now, come back in ten years and take delivery.' And the man asked, 'Morning or afternoon?' And the man behind the counter said, 'Well, ten years from now, what difference does it make?' 'Well,' the man answered, 'the plumber's coming in the morning.'"

The Associated Press, November 1, 1988, reported that Reagan told one joke he said he'd relayed to Soviet leader Mikhail Gorbachev, who, Reagan added, "laughed quite heartily":

"An American and a Russian are arguing about their two countries. And the American said, 'Look, I can go into the Oval Office, pound the President's desk, and say, "Mr. President, I don't like the way you're running our country."'

"And the Russian said, 'I can do that.'

"And the American said, 'You can?'

"And the Russian said, 'I can go into the Kremlin, into the general secretary's office, I can pound on his desk and say, "Mr. General Secretary, I don't like the way President Reagan's running his country."'"

~

The Associated Press, November 1, 1988, said Reagan claimed Gorbachev chuckled at this one, as well:

"You know, less than one family out of seven in the Soviet Union owns an automobile. Most of the automobiles are driven by the bureaucrats — the government furnishes them and drivers and so forth.

"So an order went out one day to the police that anyone caught speeding — anyone, no matter who — gets a ticket.

"Well, Gorbachev came out of his country home, his dacha; he was late getting to the Kremlin. There was his limousine and driver waiting.

"He told the driver to get in the backseat, he'd drive. And down the road he went.

"They passed two motorcycle cops. One took out after him, and pretty soon he's back with his buddy. And his buddy says, 'Well, did you give him a ticket?' And his buddy says, 'No.'

"'Well,' he said, 'why not?'

"'Oh,' the cop said, 'too important.'

"'Well,' his buddy said, 'we're told to give anybody a ticket, no matter who it is.'

"'Oh,' the cop said, 'no, no. This one was — too important, I couldn't.'"

"'Well,' the buddy said, 'who was it?'

"'I couldn't recognize him,' the cop said, 'but his driver was Gorbachev.'"

~

Reuters reported on December 11, 1987, that Reagan declared he meant what he said when in his first press conference as President in 1981 he accused Soviet leaders of reserving the right to lie and cheat to further their aims:

"And it was true . . . that there was a philosophy then under the previous leaders that there was no immorality in anything that furthered the cause of socialism, therefore permitting themselves to violate trust, to lie, and so forth."

⤳

The *Chicago Tribune* reported January 12, 1990, that Reagan was interviewed on the "Larry King Live" show and that when asked if he thought Gorbachev could be a successful politician in the United States, Reagan answered:

"Yes, because I think he is a likable person. You find yourself liking him."

Reagan Pays Tribute

Reagan once said, "I've always felt that heroes were very important to our nation. They bind us together; they give us strength that we can do great things. I felt that part of my job as President was to let our people know how many heroes we had in this country." Reagan was always quick to thank a dear friend and to praise an American hero. He received countless letters from people all over the country while in office and liked to share some of the stories he came across about some of the lesser-known heroes in this country.

In his remarks at the Republican National Committee's 1994 gala on the occasion of his eighty-third birthday in Washington, D.C., on February 3, 1994, he acknowledged some people who were important to him — his friends:

"Birthdays often serve as the rare moments when we can pause from the bustle of our daily lives to reflect on the years that have passed, the accomplishments and people that have made them special. As I look around this gathering, I am filled with countless warm and fond memories. Many of you go back with us as far as my two terms as California governor. Others of you are more recent additions to the family. Regardless of when you came, you have been a big part of our lives. For that, we are so grateful and feel so blessed."

≈

In Reagan's toast at a St. Patrick's Day luncheon hosted by the Irish ambassador on March 17, 1981, he said:

"Senator Laxalt presented me with a great big green button that he thought I should wear, which said, 'Honorary Irishman.' And I said to that son of the Basques, 'I'm not honorary; I am.'"

≈

On February 3, 1994, at the Republican National Committee's gala on the occasion of his eighty-third birthday in Washington, D.C., Reagan praised one of his most important political allies:

"Margaret Thatcher is one of the giants of our century. Her many achievements will be appreciated more and more as time goes on and history is written. For me, she has been a staunch ally, my political soul mate, a great visionary, and a dear, dear friend."

≈

Reagan recalled a time when he called former Speaker of the House Tip O'Neill regarding an issue Reagan thought they agreed upon:

"I said, 'Tip, I thought we had something going here.' And Tip said, 'Well, old buddy, that's politics. We're only friends after six P.M.' Sometimes when he came to see me, I'd set my watch up so that it would be six."

～

He also recollected the comfort he and Nancy tried to give families:

"I can't remember which memorial service it was — either this one or the ceremony for the crew of the Stark or the one for the astronauts. But Nancy and I were going from person to person trying to help with the grief, and I came to a little boy. As I took his small hand, he said to me, 'Please bring my daddy home.' I cannot describe to you the anguish."

～

"I received a message from the father of a marine in Lebanon. He told me, 'In a world where we speak of human rights, there is a sad lack of acceptance of responsibility for the privilege of living in this country.

"'My son has chosen the acceptance of responsibility for the privilege of living in the country. Certainly in this country one does not inherently have rights unless the responsibility for those rights is accepted.'"

～

"I have received some letters from the families of some of those who were on that Korean airliner that the Soviets brutally destroyed:

"One was from a mother whose twenty-eight-year-old daughter was on the plane. She had lost her husband the year before through a terrible illness. Her daughter had two children. So now the grandmother had to tell those two children that their mother was dead.

"And so she told me how the little six-year-old boy turned without a word, and then a short while later came back and handed her a drawing he had made of a little boy crying, and said, 'That's how I feel.'

"I sometimes think that if it would do any good, I'd like to send a lot of those letters to Mr. Andropov."

∾

"A grade-school class in Somerville, Massachusetts, recently wrote me to say, 'We studied about countries and found out that each country in our world is beautiful and that we need each other. People may look a little different, but we're still people who need the same things.'

"They said, 'We want peace. We want to take care of one another. We want to be able to get along with one another. We want to be able to share. We want freedom and justice. We want to be friends. We want no wars. We want to be able to talk with one another. We want to be able to travel around the world without fear.'

"And they asked, 'Do you think that we can have these things one day?'

"Well, I do. I really do. Simple wishes may seem far from fulfillment. But we can achieve them. We must never stop trying."

∾

"A private citizen in Louisiana asked the government for help in developing his property. He received back a letter that said, 'We have observed that you have not traced the title prior to 1803. Before final approval, it will be necessary that the title be traced previous to that year.' Well, the citizen's answer was eloquent.

"'Gentlemen,' he wrote, 'I am unaware that any educated man failed to know that Louisiana was purchased from France in 1803. The title of the land was acquired by France by right of conquest from Spain. The land came into the possession of Spain in 1492 by right of discovery by an Italian sailor, Christopher Columbus. The good Queen Isabella took the precaution of receiving the blessing of the Pope. . . . The Pope is emissary of the Son of God, who made this world.

"'Therefore, I believe that it is safe to assume that He also made that part of the United States called Louisiana. And I hope to hell you're satisfied.'"

≈

"One Ohio businessman writes to us about his personal frustration with burdensome regulations. He cites an item from the Toledo Area Small Business Association bulletin.

"'It is reported to us,' the item read, 'that the Lord's Prayer contains 57 words. Lincoln's Gettysburg address has 266 words. The Ten Commandments are presented in just 297 words, and the Declaration of Independence has only 300 words.'

"And then it goes on to say, 'An Agriculture Department order setting the price of cabbage has 26,911 words.'"

≈

"Another letter was addressed: 'To aide opening this letter. I didn't vote for you. I voted for Ronald Reagan, and I want him to read this letter.'

"And I read it!

"The lady said, 'I am a farm wife, sixty years old, not too well educated, but it doesn't take too smart a person to see and feel what's going on. I know you have a lot of things to do and decide, but have you ever stopped and thought about the farmers?

"'Stop and think: Can a farmer pay seventy-five to one hundred thousand dollars for a combine? Can he pay the price for fertilizer, seed, you name it, and sell corn, wheat, and soybeans for the price they are today?'

"She said, 'Just because farmers aren't out carrying strike signs or tearing something up doesn't mean they're not hurting. What farmers want is a fair price so they can pay their bills and feed their families.'

"She was only wrong about one thing, that maybe I hadn't time to think about farmers. The farmers of America are very much on my mind."

~

"I received a call from a union worker, before the 1981 Solidarity Day March in Washington, to tell me that he not only wasn't going to go but to read me a copy of the letter he had sent to the head of his union explaining why the union shouldn't go and why they should be in support of what we're trying to do. The courage of that man was thrilling and exciting."

~

"And then came a letter from a sixteen-year-old boy who said, 'From what's going on there, I'm sure that you're going to save the country for kids like me.'"

~

"A lady down in New Orleans wrote to tell me that she was black, she told me her age — I won't reveal it here, but she was very elderly — and then she told me, 'Thanks for destroying the war on poverty. Maybe now we can get back to growing our own muscles and taking care of ourselves the way we should.'"

∾

"A letter came from a lady in Illinois who told me that she was one of three CETA employees at the time when we were changing that program. She said, 'I just want you to know that there is only work enough for one of us. We don't need three. As we came to the end of the last fiscal year, there was money left over.'

"She continued, 'I was ordered to go out and buy new office furniture because we couldn't have money left over or the grant money might be reduced for the coming year. So here I sit at my great new executive desk with nothing to do.'

"Well, I thought that was too much, so I called in some of my staff, read them the letter, and said, 'She deserves better than she's got.' And you know something? She is now employed in a twenty-five-thousand-a-year job out in the private sector and happy with her work.

"She says it sure beats daytime TV."

∾

"Received a letter from a retiree the other day. It contained his check for civil service retirement, a full month's retirement endorsed over to the Treasury Department because he said he just wanted to help us get the job done."

∾

"This letter had to be translated from Braille. A GI who had lost his sight in World War Two in Germany wrote, in Braille, to tell me that if cutting his pension would help get this country back on its feet, he'd like to have me cut his pension.

"Well, we're not going to cut his pension. But we are going to get this country back on its feet."

~

The *Des Moines Register and Tribune* invited grade-school children to write letters to the paper advising the President on his job:

"One eleven-year-old boy wrote, 'When you get there, don't look to the past, look to the future. You won't have time to look to the past. Make up your mind that when you leave there you will be older and tired, and there will be a few more gray hairs on your wise old head.'

"And then he said, 'Just get to the office, go to work, and be happy that you're only the President, you don't have to be God.'

"Out of the mouths of babes."

Passing the Torch

Perhaps one of Reagan's greatest and most generous tributes was to George Bush, who had come to the White House as Reagan's Vice President, and who ran for President on the Republican ticket in 1988.

August 12, 1988:

"What do American people believe in? Teaching right from wrong, putting criminals behind bars and keeping them there — and promoting excellence in education, and saying the Pledge of Allegiance, America's tradition of peace through strength, and upholding the Monroe Doctrine — this is also what we believe in. And that's one reason why the American people are going to vote with us this November and why we're going to hold the White House with George Bush."

≈

"I wanted to do all I could to see that the policies we'd set in motion in 1981 would continue. During the primaries, I'd had to follow the Eleventh Commandment and remain neutral. But once George won the nomination, I did all I could to help him get elected. I knew George would be a great President."

≈

After one of Bush's televised debates, Reagan said:

"Now you all know the man I'm rooting for in the presidential election: that silver-tongued devil George Bush. I could have told the other guy not to get into a fight with George. After all, look what happened when George fought for America in World War Two — fifty-eight combat missions completed. And I guess you could say that last week George Bush completed his fifty-ninth, and it sure was a bull's-eye."

≈

In his autobiography *An American Life,* Reagan wrote about the final trip to the Oval Office that he made on the morning of George Bush's inauguration:

"On January 20 [1988], I got up earlier than usual and did some last-minute puttering in my study, then went over to the Oval Office.

"Alone in the office, I wrote a note to George Bush and stuck it in the top drawer of the desk that in a few hours would become his. I wrote the note on a little pad of paper with a printed heading: DON'T LET THE TURKEYS GET YOU DOWN. It said:

Dear George,

You'll have moments when you want to use this particular stationery. Well, go for it.

George, I treasure the memories we share and wish you all the very best. You'll be in my prayers. God bless you and Barbara. I'll miss our Thursday lunches.

Ron

Saying Good-bye

In the end, Reagan left the White House proud of his eight years in office:

"And how stands the city on this winter night? More prosperous, more secure, and happier than it was eight years ago. But more than that; after two hundred years, two centuries, she still stands strong and true on the granite ridge, and her glow has held steady no matter what storm. And she's still a beacon, still a magnet for all who must have freedom, for all the pilgrims from all the lost places who are hurtling through the darkness, towards home. We've done our part. And as I walk off into the city streets, a final word to the men and women of the Reagan Revolution, the men and women across America who for eight years did the work that brought America back. My friends: we did it. We weren't just marking time. We made a difference. We made the city stronger. We made the city freer, and we left her in good hands. All in all, not bad, not bad at all."

〜

Looking back on his days in office, Reagan said on his eighty-third birthday:

"When we came to Washington on that bright sunny day in January of 1981, we shared a dream for America. Back then, the reach of government had become intolerable. It was a time of rampant inflation and crushing interest rates — when hope was scarce. It was a time when cold, ugly walls divided nations and human rights were trampled in the name of evil and corrupt ideologies. It was a time when the nuclear arms race was spiraling out of control and a blinding mistrust stood between East and West. We believed that for the future of America and the free world, this could not stand."

~

When the Reagans arrived at the White House in 1981, the Carters made a quick exit, which offended the new President and his wife. But when it was their turn to leave, Reagan was more understanding of his predecessor's departure:

"At the time, Nancy and I took [their sudden departure] as an affront. It seemed rude. But eight years later I think we could sense a little of how President Carter must have felt that day — to have served as President, to have been through the intense highs and lows of the job, to have tried to do what he thought was right, to have had all the farewells, good-bye parties, and then to be forced out of the White House by a vote of the people. . . . It must have been very hard on him. One of the great things about America is how smoothly we transfer presidential power, but after having lived in the White House, and having left it, I can understand how sad it must have been for Jimmy and Rosalynn Carter that day."

∼

At the Republican National Committee's 1994 gala on the occasion of his eighty-third birthday in Washington, D.C., on February 3, 1994, Reagan said:

"In our America, most people still believed in the power of a better tomorrow. So together we got the government off the backs of the American people. We created millions of new jobs for Americans at all income levels. We cut taxes and freed the people from the shackles of too much government. And the economy burst loose in the longest peacetime expansion ever. We brought America back — bigger and better than ever."

THE REAGAN HUMOR

Part of Reagan's ability to bring the country together in both good times and bad had to do with his ability to make us laugh. Reagan not only understood the power laughter had over a crowd, but he let audiences see his own laughter and sense of humor, which created a bridge between himself and an audience.

On Washington

Once Reagan moved to Washington, he couldn't help but poke fun at his new hometown and the political life in general:

"I know you've been reading a lot about what's going on here in Washington. Some of it is true."

≈

Reagan often quoted the great American writer and humorist Mark Twain:

"We've been trying to follow the advice of Mark Twain, which was, 'Do what's right and you'll please some of the people and astound the rest.'"

≈

"I don't know of any place where prayer is more needed than in Washington, D.C."

≈

"When you mention common sense in Washington, you cause traumatic shock."

～

"In Washington people don't realize that you can't drink yourself sober or spend yourself rich; that you can't prime the pump without pumping the prime."

～

"Probably the most accurate description of the American Revolution was given to me by an Englishman, who said they understood it was just an argument between groups of Englishmen."

～

Remarks at the presentation ceremony for the "C" Flag Awards on September 29, 1988:

"Today there are some forty-five hundred 'C' flags waving across America. And I have to confess: I'm a guy who loves to wave the flag. Partly, that's because Betsy Ross and I were childhood friends."

～

One of Ronald Reagan's trademarks was the jar of jelly beans he had on the table during cabinet meetings:

"Sometimes when a cabinet meeting starts to drag, I wonder what would happen if the jar on the table was filled with jalapeño jelly beans."

～

"There are two ways of doing things: the right way, and the way they do it in Washington."

~

"I had an uncle who was a Democrat in Chicago. He received a silver cup from the party for voting fifteen straight elections — he'd been dead for fourteen of them."

~

"Where else but in Washington could they call the department that's in charge of everything outside and out-of-doors the Department of the Interior."

~

In his remarks to the graduating class of Glassboro High School in New Jersey on June 19, 1986, Reagan told students:

"But there are advantages to being elected President. The day after I was elected, I had my high-school grades classified as Top Secret."

~

Of course the First Family's busy schedule was worthy of a joke:

"Let me say on behalf of Nancy, who couldn't be here but wanted to be — she has a schedule too. I used to just come home, open the front door, and say, 'I'm home.' Now I come home, look through a hundred and thirty-two rooms, and then look at her schedule — to know where she is."

~

During Reagan's second term, the press made much of the tensions between the First Lady and the White House chief of staff, Donald Regan. Naturally, Reagan made light of it to the press:

"Nancy and Don at one point tried to patch things up. They met privately over lunch. Just the two of them and their food tasters."

Reagan Laughs at Reagan

Part of Reagan's charm was that in addition to having a wonderful sense of humor about the world around him, he could also laugh at himself and invited the world to laugh with him. And when opponents tried to exploit his age as a weakness, he was quick to make a joke — letting his wit show that his mind was still sharp as a tack.

"It's true hard work never killed anybody, but I figure why take the chance."

∽

During his remarks to employees at the Chrysler Corporation of St. Louis assembly plant in Fenton, Missouri, on February 1, 1983, he said:

"I just wanted you to know, I'm not above stealing a good line when I hear one."

∽

According to a story in the *Courier-Journal,* April 14, 1989, that reported on Washington's annual soiree of satire, the Gridiron Club banquet, Reagan of course gave his share:

"I heard one presidential candidate say that what this country needed was a President for the nineties. I was set to run again. I thought he said a President in his nineties."

≈

In his remarks at the presentation ceremony for the President's Volunteer Action Awards on April 13, 1983, he said:

"I don't know how many of you stayed up the other night to watch the Academy Awards. I broke a rule and stayed up past midnight. They never called my name."

≈

"There was a Democrat during the campaign who told a large group, 'Don't worry, I've seen Ronald Reagan, and he looks like a million.'

"He was talking about my age."

≈

"Not too long ago Senator Kennedy paid a tribute to former governor and ambassador Averell Harriman, who was celebrating a birthday in his nineties. Kennedy said that Ambassador Harriman's age was only one-half as old as Ronald Reagan's ideas.

"Well, you know, he's absolutely right! The United States Constitution is almost two hundred years old, and that's where I'm proud to get my ideas."

≈

At the congressional barbecue on September 15, 1988, he said:

"Just for the record, I'm speaking in jest here. Of course, some of you think I've been doing that for eight years."

～

To the winners of the Bicentennial of the Constitution National Essay Contest on September 10, 1987:

"History's no easy subject. Even in my day it wasn't, and we had so much less of it to learn then."

～

During his remarks at the Republican National Convention in New Orleans, Louisiana, on August 15, 1988, Reagan said:

"This convention brings back so many memories to a fellow like me. I can still remember my first Republican convention: Abraham Lincoln giving a speech that sent tingles down my spine. No, I have to confess, I wasn't actually there. The truth is, way back then, I belonged to the other party."

～

Remarks on signing the Omnibus Trade and Competitiveness Act in 1988 in Long Beach, California, on August 23, 1988:

"Of course, when you're my age, everything brings back memories — even other memories."

～

During the presentation ceremony for the "C" Flag Awards on September 29, 1988, Reagan began telling a story which he admitted to telling more than once. He remarked:

"But at my age people aren't surprised when you start repeating yourself. Of course I've been repeating myself for so many years now that it would be risky to stop — because then some people would say, 'Hey, I guess he's losing his memory.'"

∼

In his remarks on signing the Alternative Motor Fuels Act of 1988 on October 14, 1988, Reagan said:

"And believe me, when you're my age, you just love hearing about alternative sources of energy."

∼

At a rally in Tampa, Florida, on October 24, 1986:

"Well, the history books tell us that one of the first visitors to Tampa was Ponce de León. He was looking for the Fountain of Youth. And, no, it's not true that I was with him. If I had been, I'd have seen that he found it."

∼

Reagan was asked about his hair and whether he had changed his style:

"I saw an article that said I had changed. They showed two different pictures of me. Well, the one was taken on a windy day outdoors, and the other one was taken with my hair combed.

"Incidentally, I just washed my hair the night before last, so it's a little fluffy right now. The only thing that happened to me was, last winter, without my realizing it, my barber was letting it get a little longer than I like. And I took him to task and said, 'Crop it the way it was.'

"It's the same haircut. I'm too old to change my haircut now."

∾

At Eureka College in Eureka, Illinois, on February 6, 1984:

"And I have what every man who has that many candles on his birthday cake needs around him — a large group of friends and a working sprinkler system."

∾

Reagan revealed a self-discovered trick with his contact lenses that helped him to see not only his notes and the TelePrompTer but everything else in life:

"I am very nearsighted in both eyes and started wearing some of the first contact lenses made in America. But a few years ago, I discovered that if I wore only one lens, nature sort of took over and, in effect, gave me bifocals. I wear a contact lens over my left eye but nothing over my right eye; the corrective lens over my left eye gives me twenty-twenty vision for seeing things over distances, while my right eye takes over at shorter range and allows me to read fine print. Everything is in balance, equalized by nature."

∾

During his remarks at a question-and-answer session with regional press representatives on February 10, 1986:

"If I'm ever in need of any transplants, I got parts they don't make anymore."

～

At the annual convention of National Religious Broadcasters on January 31, 1983:

"In a few days I'll be celebrating another birthday, which, according to some in the press, puts me on par with Moses."

～

In a question-and-answer session with reporters on domestic and foreign policy issues on February 4, 1983, one of the reporters asked the President what he felt about being seventy-two years old. Reagan answered:

"I think that it's fine when you consider the alternative."

～

To students and faculty at Thomas Jefferson High School in Fairfax, Virginia, on February 7, 1986:

"Believe it or not, I can remember my first ride in an automobile. Most of the time it'd been horse and buggy. The horse was very fuel-efficient but kind of slow. If you wanted to supercharge one, you fed him an extra bag of oats."

～

His toast to Prime Minister Menachem Begin of Israel on September 9, 1981, said:

"You will hear no criticism of age tolerated in this house. Lately, I've been heartened to remember that Moses was eighty when God commissioned him for public service, and he lived to be a hundred and twenty. And Abraham was a hundred and his wife, Sarah, ninety, when they did something truly amazing."

∾

At a signing ceremony for the legislative agenda and the economic report of the President on February 6, 1986, Reagan said:

"I did turn seventy-five today, but remember, that's only twenty-four Celsius."

∾

Reagan told his colleagues at the annual Salute to Congress Dinner on February 4, 1981:

"I can define middle-aged. That's when you're faced with two temptations and you choose the one that'll get you home at nine o'clock."

∾

"In the business I used to be in, if you didn't sing or dance, you wound up as an after-dinner speaker — so here I am."

∾

In his remarks to employees of the Department of Health and Human Services on February 5, 1986:

"I always think age is relative. There was once a very famous baseball pitcher, Satchel Paige. And no one knew quite how old Satchel was, but he was still throwing that ball. And somebody asked him about that, and his wise answer was, 'How old would you be if you didn't know how old you were?' That's how I came up with thirty-nine. Well, the late Jack Benny had something to do with that. He was thirty-nine for more than forty years."

≈

Remarks at the welcoming rally at the Republican National Convention in New Orleans, Louisiana, on August 14, 1988:

"I always feel at home here in Louisiana because, you know, I'm the fella that talked Tom Jefferson into buying it."

≈

During Reagan's remarks to employees of the Department of the Treasury on February 5, 1986, regarding his birthday, he said:

"I prefer to think of it as the thirty-sixth anniversary of my thirty-ninth. A few more of these and I'll be ready for a midlife crisis. In fact, I'm thinking about a career change. Drop this political business and see if I can't do something different, like radio or the movies."

≈

The *Los Angeles Times* reported on June 4, 1988, that Reagan joked about his age while speaking in London's fifteenth-century Guildhall:

"It is comforting to be near anything that much older than myself. Some even see my election to the presidency as America's attempt to show our European cousins that we too have a regard for antiquity."

~

"For years, I've heard the question: 'How could an actor be President?' I've sometimes wondered how you could be President and not be an actor."

Playing the Crowd

Reagan's habit of speaking informally to the crowd before he delivered a speech often charmed and amused his audience.

In his address at commencement exercises at the University of Notre Dame on May 17, 1981, Reagan quipped:

"My first time to ever see Notre Dame was to come here as a sports announcer, two years out of college, to broadcast a football game. You won or I wouldn't have mentioned it."

~

To a crowd in Minnesota:

"I feel very much at home here in your lovely farm and dairy country. I'm a rancher myself. I take a little kidding now and then in Washington about our ranch."

"But you know, even some Midwesterners admit that cattle fit right into the California scene. They stand around all day in the sun, no clothes on, eating salad.

"I just want to assure you that cows in California are the same as cows in Minnesota. Except, of course, in California they have their teeth capped."

～

He remarked during a visit to Walt Disney World's EPCOT Center near Orlando, Florida, on March 8, 1983:

"I'm very happy to see so many young people here today, the math and science whizzes of central Florida, plus the students participating in the World Showcase Fellowship Program. And you adults are welcome too.

"I just watched a program — I don't know just what to call it — a show, a pageant, with several hundred of my junior high and high school friends here, and I'm pleased to announce I didn't get hit with one spitball."

～

Reagan said to the St. Louis Regional Commerce and Growth Association in Missouri on February 1, 1983:

"Just a few weeks ago in Illinois, a group of road builders met with me and gave me a hard hat — which I expect to use in my dealings with Congress this session."

～

During his remarks to the employees of United States Precision Lens, in Cincinnati, Ohio, on August 8, 1988, Reagan teased:

"You know, I can't tell you how good it feels to come here to the heartland, where America's work gets done, and to get away from the puzzle palace on the Potomac. Every time I leave Washington to travel around the country, as I get out of the plane I half expect to see a sign waiting for me saying, 'Welcome to America.' You know, if I didn't get out of Washington often, it would be easy to lose touch with what's really going on. Back at the airport someone asked me my impressions of the Reds' manager. I told him, but I still don't know if he meant Pete Rose or Gorbachev."

~

Reagan, back in a grammar-school classroom after many decades, commented:

"I thought maybe you asked me here to remedial English class because you heard my speeches."

~

Mr. Reagan was speaking to a large audience, and a few demonstrators in the back of the room were shouting, trying to interrupt him. The President ignored them for a bit, and then:

"You know, I spoke here in 1975, and there wasn't an echo."

~

At the Republican National Committee gala on February 3, 1994, Reagan said:

"After watching the State of the Union address the other night, I'm reminded of the old adage that imitation is the sincerest form of flattery. Only in this case, it's not flattery, but grand larceny: the intellectual theft of ideas that you and I recognize as our own. Speech delivery counts for little on the world stage unless you have convictions, and, yes, the vision to see beyond the front-row seats."

~

In addition to charming a crowd on his own, Reagan was comfortable falling into banter with an old friend onstage. Reagan was on hand at the fortieth anniversary of the USO and also Bob Hope's association with the USO. The two men traded one-liners all night. Here are a few of the President's:

"I don't think any of us realize that there probably isn't anyone who loves his work as much as Bob Hope.

"I discovered that once when he was up at our ranch and I took him over to show him our horses. Then I got a telephone call. When I came back he was doing a monologue to the horses. And they were laughing.

"Of course his other love is golf. When we met tonight, I said, 'Hello, how are you?' And he said, 'Hello, what's your handicap?' I said, 'The Congress.'"

The Teller of Tales

Ronald Reagan was a great American President, and he was also a masterful storyteller. In fact, it's impossible to separate Reagan the President from Reagan the storyteller. Here are a few of the President's favorites.

Reagan once told a story about an old preacher who was giving some advice to a young preacher:

"He said, 'You know, sometimes on Sunday morning they'll begin to nod off.' And he says, 'I've found a way to wake them up. Right in my sermon when I see them begin to doze, I say, "Last night I held in my arms a woman who is the wife of another man." Then, when they look at me, startled, I say, "It was my dear mother."

"Well, the young preacher took that to heart, and a few weeks later, sure enough, some in the congregation were dozing off. He remembered the advice, and he said, 'Last night I held in my arms the wife of another man.' They all looked at him, and everyone was awake. And he says, 'I can't remember who it was.'"

~

"A fellow fell off a cliff. As he was falling, he grabbed a limb sticking out the side of the cliff and looked down three hundred feet to the canyon floor below. Then he looked up and said, 'Lord, if there's anyone up there, give me faith. Tell me what to do. And a voice from the heavens said, 'If you have faith, let go.' He looked down to the canyon floor and then took another look up and said, 'Is there anyone else up there?'"

~

"Some politicians are kind of like the two campers who were hiking and spotted a grizzly bear coming over the hill, headed right for them.

"One of them reached into his pack as quick as he could, pulled out a pair of tennis shoes, sat down, and started putting on the tennis shoes.

"The other looked at him and said, 'You don't mean you think you can outrun a grizzly?'"

"The fellow with the tennis shoes stood up and said, 'I don't have to outrun the grizzly; I just have to outrun you.'"

∼

Mr. Reagan was speaking in the tenth-anniversary gathering of the Organization of Executive Women in Government:

"There was an accident one day; the victim was lying there, and bystanders had gathered around.

"A woman was bending over him trying to help. A man came elbowing his way through the bystanders, shoved the woman aside, and said, 'Let me at him. I have first-aid training.'

"She stepped aside, and he knelt down and started doing the prescribed things in his training. At one point she tapped him on the shoulder and said, 'When you get to the part about calling the doctor, I'm right here.'"

∼

"And then there was Lincoln. As a young lawyer he once had to plead two cases in the same day before the same judge. Both involved the same principle of law. But in one Lincoln appeared for the defendant and in the other for the plaintiff.

"Now, you can see how this makes anything above a fifty percent success rate very difficult.

"In the morning Lincoln made an eloquent plea and won his case. Later he took the opposite side and was arguing just as earnestly.

"Puzzled, the judge asked why the change of attitude. 'Your Honor,' said Honest Abe, 'I may have been wrong in the morning . . . but now I know I'm right now.'"

~

"An evangelical minister and a politician arrived at heaven's gate one day together. Saint Peter, after handling all the formalities, took them in hand to show them where their new quarters would be. He took them to a small, single room with a bed, a chair, and a table, and said this was for the clergyman.

"Well, the politician was a little worried about what might be in store for him. He couldn't believe it when Saint Peter stopped in front of a beautiful mansion with lovely grounds and many servants and told him that these would be his quarters.

"The politician couldn't help but ask, 'But wait — there's something wrong. How do I get a mansion while that good and holy man gets a single room?'

"And Saint Peter said, 'You have to understand how things are up here. We've got thousands and thousands of clergy. You're the first politician who ever made it.'"

~

"I can remember when there weren't so many Republicans in California, when not too long ago Republicans seemed as plentiful as spring water in Death Valley. And I speak with authority because I spent a good chunk of my life on that piece of real estate.

"Then there was the Mississippi Republican, the first to try for a seat in this southern district. He dropped in on a farm there, and told the farmer he was a Republican candidate for Congress in the district.

"The farmer's eyes popped open, his jaw dropped, and he said, 'Wait right here just a minute.' He went running across the barnyard yelling, 'Ma, Ma.' She came out, and back the two of them came hand in hand. They stood in front of him and said, 'We've never seen a Republican before. Would you make a speech?'

"Well, he looked around for some sort of platform. The only thing he could see there was a pile of stuff that it took the late Bess Truman thirty-five years to get Harry to call fertilizer. Anyway, he climbed up on it and made his speech.

"When he stepped down, they said it was the first time they had ever heard a Republican speech. He said, 'Well, that's all right. That's the first time I've ever given a speech from a Democratic platform.'"

~

Reagan remembered a preacher friend of his from Oklahoma who taught him the lesson of brevity in a speech:

"The preacher recalled his first appearance in the pulpit. He had worked for weeks on his first sermon, which he was to give at an evening service in a little country church.

"Well, he stood up in the pulpit that night and looked out at an empty church, except for one little lone fellow sitting down there in all the empty pews.

"So after the music, he went down and said, 'Look, my friend, I'm just a young preacher getting started. You seem to be the only member of the congregation who showed up. What about it, should I go through with it?'

"The fellow said, 'Well, I'm a little old cowpoke out here in Oklahoma. I don't know much about that sort of thing, but I do know this: if I loaded up a truckload of hay, took it out to the prairie, and only one cow showed up, I'd feed her.'

"The preacher took that as a cue, got back up in the pulpit, and an hour and a half later said, 'Amen.' He then went back down and said, 'My friend, you seem to have stuck with me. And like I told you, I'm a young preacher getting started. Tell me what you thought.'

"'Well,' he says, 'like I told you, I don't know about that sort of thing, but I do know this: if I loaded up a truckload of hay, took it out on the prairie, and only one cow showed up, I sure wouldn't feed her the whole load.'"

≈

During his remarks at the annual meeting of the National Alliance of Business on October 5, 1981, Reagan said:

"I heard of a fellow who had been unemployed for a long time, and a few days ago he found a job at a china warehouse. He'd only worked there a couple of days when he smashed a large oriental vase. The boss told him in no uncertain terms that the money would be deducted from his wages every week until the vase was paid for. And the fellow asked, 'How much did it cost?' He told him three hundred dollars. And the fellow cheered and said, 'At last, I've found steady work.'"

≈

Reagan liked to tell this story about three brothers, a lawyer, a doctor, and an engineer, who were too cheap to pay for a vacation for their retired parents, who had sacrificed in order to finance their children's education:

"Do you realize that your mother and I were so busy working, trying to save money, that we never took time out to get a marriage license?" the exasperated father asked them. At which point, the three sons gasped in unison. "Father, do you know what that makes us?" Their father responded, "Yes, and cheap ones, too."

∾

"I take a lot of ribbing for praising silent Cal Coolidge, but he was a real communicator.

"He was having his hair cut once in a one-chair barbershop up in Vermont, and the town doctor came in, sat down, and said, 'Cal, did you take the pills I gave you?' Coolidge said nothing for a minute or two, then in his usual articulate style he said, 'Nope.' A little later the doctor asked, 'Well, are you feeling any better?' Another long silence and then he said, 'Yup.'

"Well, his haircut was finished, and he started to leave. The barber hesitantly said, 'Aren't you forgetting something?' An embarrassed Coolidge replied, 'Oh, yeah, I'm sorry. I forgot to pay you. I was so busy gossiping with the doctor, it slipped my mind.'"

∾

Reagan had another favorite about his hero Cal:

"Some of you may know that after Cal Coolidge was introduced to the sport of fishing by his Secret Service detail, it got to be quite a passion with him, if you can use that word about 'Silent Cal.' Anyway, he was once asked by reporters how many fish were in one of his favorite angling places, the River Brule. And Coolidge said the waters were estimated to carry forty-five thousand trout. And then he said, 'I haven't caught them all yet, but I sure have intimidated them.'"

~

"The third-grade teacher was trying to impress on her students that winter had come along, and she was trying to tell them how to avoid colds. She told a very heartrending tale about her little brother.

"As the story went, her little brother was a fun-loving boy, and he went out on his sled, stayed out too long, caught cold, then pneumonia, and three days later he was dead.

"When she finished with the tale, there was silence in the room. She thought she had really gotten through to them when a voice in the back said, 'Where's his sled?'"

~

"Every time I talk about intelligence and wisdom, I think of the old legend of the three wise men on the island that was threatened with being flooded by a hurricane.

"One of them decided that in the limited time left he would do all the things he had never been able to do in his life.

"The second one devoted himself to further study.

"The third one was a good pattern for everyone. He retreated with his closest advisers to the highest point on the island and set out to determine whether they could live under water."

~

"Many years ago, in the days of the austerity in England just after the Labour government had gotten in, I arrived for the royal command performance at the Savoy Hotel.

"I went down to the dining room. There was rationing, and you couldn't get food such as we have today; but then on the menu I saw pheasant. And I thought, well, you can't go wrong if you order pheasant, so I ordered it.

"But I didn't know about their custom of serving game birds. Well, the waiter came out and with a flourish removed the lid, and I was looking at a bird that was looking back at me: the head and the ruff were on, the eyes were open, and the big yellow legs were attached to him. It did curb my appetite a little.

"The following day another American arrived and ordered the pheasant. I watched, without saying a word, the same flourish from the waiter, and there was the bird, staring back.

"As the waiter started away, the American grabbed him by the coattail, saying, 'Bring me liniment, and I'll have the bird flying again in fifteen minutes.'"

⌀

Reagan rarely resisted an opportunity to tell one of Mark Twain's tales:

"Mark Twain was on a steamer going across to Europe. In the dining salon one night at dinner, someone at the table who wanted to impress him asked him to pass the sugar and then said, 'Mr. Twain, don't you think it's unusual that sugar is the only word in our language in which s-u has the *shu* sound?'

And Twain said, 'Are you sure?'"

~

"There was a Texan visiting a farm up in Maine. The Texan asked this old boy about his farm and what might be the extent of his spread.

"The old fellow said, 'Well, it runs to that clump of trees and then over to that hill and then down to the creek and over to there. How big is your spread in Texas?'

"The Texan looked at him and said, 'Well, old-timer, sometimes I get in my car and drive for an hour and a half before I get to the boundary of my farm.'

"The old fellow from Maine looked at him for a minute and then said, 'I know what you mean. I had a car like that myself once.'"

~

Reagan, speaking to students participating in International Youth Exchange Programs:

"Just after World War Two, I was in England. One weekend I went out to the countryside to see one of the fabulous ancient pubs. The driver apologized when he stopped at one that was about four hundred years old — he hadn't been able to find a really old one.

"Well, we went in; it was a mom-and-pop operation — you know, the old gentleman at the bar and a matronly woman. She came in and took our order. After hearing us for a few seconds, she said, 'You're Americans, aren't you?' I allowed as how we were. She said, 'Oh, there were a lot of your chaps stationed down the road during the war. They used to come in and hold songfests. They called me Mom, and they called the old boy Pop.'

"She continued on. 'It was Christmas Eve' — and by this time she's not looking at us anymore; she's kind of looking off into the distance, and her eyes are beginning to fill up — 'it was Christmas Eve, and we were here all alone, and in they all came. And they had presents, Christmas presents for me and Pop.'

By this time the tears were rolling down her cheeks. She managed: 'Big strappin' lads, they was, from a place called Ioway.'"

~

"The thing I like about speaking before doctors is that you generate as many anecdotes as do politicians . . .

"Like the one about the fellow who went to the hospital for a complete checkup, very depressed, and said to the doctor, 'I look in the mirror, I'm a mess. My jowls are sagging. I have blotches all over my face. My hair has fallen out. I feel ugly. What is it?' And the doctor said, 'I don't know what it is, but your eyesight is perfect.'"

~

Reagan once told this story to a small group of White House visitors. Imagine the story told in the former movie star's voice and tempo:

"A couple were sleeping as guests in Abraham Lincoln's bedroom. They were visitors more than once at the White House. And one morning the lady came forth and said that she had awakened and saw a figure standing down at the foot of the bed and looking out the windows. And when that figure turned, it was Abraham Lincoln.

"She said she swore by it. And he — the figure — then left the room. Well, her husband just couldn't believe it. He said, 'Oh, you must have been dreaming.' And believe it or not, sometime later he was almost on his knees apologizing to his wife because he had awakened and he saw a figure standing down at the other end of the room and saw that figure leave and go through the door."

∿

This was one of Reagan's favorite stories about optimism:

"A man had two sons, and he was very disturbed about them. One was a pessimist beyond recall, and the other was an optimist beyond reason. He talked to a child psychiatrist, who made a suggestion. He said, 'I think we can fix that. We'll get a room, and we'll fill it with the most wonderful toys any boy ever had. And we'll put the pessimist in, and when he finds out the toys are for him, he'll get over being a pessimist.'

"The father said, 'What will you do about the optimist?' 'Well,' he said, 'I have a friend who has a racing stable, and they clean out the stalls every morning. And,' he said, 'I can get quite an amount of that substance. We'll put that in another room, and when the optimist who's seen his brother get all the toys is then shown his own room, he'll get over it.'

"Well, they showed each boy his room and waited five minutes. When they opened the door the pessimist was crying as if his heart would break. He said, 'I know that somebody's going to come in and take these away from me.'

"Then they went down to the other room and opened the door, and there was the kid, happy as a clam, throwing that stuff over his shoulder as fast as he could. They said, 'What are you doing?' and he said, 'There's got to be a pony in here somewhere.'"

LIFE AFTER THE PRESIDENCY

Remarks by Reagan at the Republican National Committee's 1994 gala on the occasion of his eighty-third birthday in Washington, D.C., on February 3, 1994:

"Well, one of the benefits of retirement is you get a chance to reflect back over the years. Since Nancy and I have returned to California, we've spent many occasions looking back at what we did here and remembering the extraordinary people who worked so hard to make those great days possible. And we've wondered if we would ever get the chance to thank them. You are those people — those great individuals who gave so much of yourselves — who sacrificed and supported us and helped us achieve everything we did. So, I will conclude tonight by saying that the greatest gift I could receive on my birthday is to be able to stand before each and every one of you and convey in the only words I can how grateful Nancy and I are: thank you for being there — and for being here. And thank you for making this evening a memory I will cherish forever. Until we meet again, God bless you, my friends."

∽

In 1987, three years before Reagan's autobiography *An American Life* was published, someone asked him what his plans were for retirement. Reagan answered:

"There has been talk of a book, and I'm seriously considering it — as an act of self-defense."

∽

Life after the Presidency

In the acknowledgments of his book *An American Life,* Reagan wrote:

"The question I am most often asked these days is whether I miss Washington. Although I enjoyed the presidency, I don't miss the job. What I do miss is the people — the good and decent people from every state in the union, from all walks of life, black and white, Christian and Jew, rich and poor, military and civilian, political and civil service, who comprise the executive offices of the president of the United States, joined only by the desire to serve their country. They do so with the greatest dedication and distinction. We miss them, we keep them in our hearts, and we will always be grateful to them."

∼

According to the *South China Morning Post,* April 4, 1994, there were some rumors going around that ex-President Reagan was learning to play the harmonica. When the *New York Times* called Reagan's Los Angeles office to check on the musical rumors, he replied with a humorous, handwritten note sent by fax:

He alluded to the fact that TV journalist Connie Chung had also called to check out the report, hoping to film a harmonica lesson for her news magazine, *Eye to Eye.* "Is this an April Fool's spoof?" Reagan asked, in his cramped handwriting on stationery engraved simply with his name and the seal of the United States. "You're the second person inquiring about my harmonica playing ability — or lack thereof.

"Unfortunately, I'm not taking music lessons and probably should be. I've always liked the harmonica, but can barely play a tune. My repertoire is limited to 'Red River Valley' and I play for my own self-amusement exclusively — usually when I don't have my hearing aids in. Thanks for thinking of me anyway. Have a blessed Easter. Sincerely, Ronald Reagan."

~

In *An American Life,* Reagan reflected not only on the importance of hard work, but on the examples of hard workers that inspired him throughout his working years:

"I learned that hard work is an essential part of life — that by and large, you don't get something for nothing — and that America was a place that offered unlimited opportunity to those who did work hard. I learned to admire risk takers and entrepreneurs, be they farmers or small merchants, who went to work and took small risks to build something for themselves and their children, pushing at the boundaries of their lives to make them better."

~

Even in his retirement, Reagan was inspired by the American people:

"I have always wondered at this American marvel, the great energy of the human soul that drives people to better themselves and improve the fortunes of their families and communities. Indeed, I know of no greater force on earth."

~

Reagan remained active in the political arena in his retirement. He gave a speech to the Republican National Committee on August 17, 1992:

" . . . the principle so eloquently stated by Abraham Lincoln: 'You cannot strengthen the weak by weakening the strong. You cannot help the wage earner by pulling down the wage payer. You cannot help the poor by destroying the rich. You cannot help men permanently by doing for them what they could and should do for themselves.'"

On Freedom

Reagan once said: "What we must all learn is that you can't lose a freedom anyplace without losing freedom every place." Throughout his life, individual freedom was a principle close to Reagan's heart. He could articulate in a way no one else could what made American freedom unique in the world and why, as a country, we needed to defend and above all cherish it. The following is a selection of some of Reagan's powerful statements on the subject.

"A group of young Americans was touring Latvia a few years ago. They were given an opportunity to visit with a local artist:

"This painter, careful with her words because she was speaking through a government interpreter, suggested that the artist fared better under communism because the system demanded quality before an artist's work could be shown, and that this prevented an underdeveloped artist from ruining his or her reputation.

"This painter, for example, said she had worked hard and was soon to be permitted a showing in Moscow. She pulled out some examples of her work, and, as is so often the case with socialist realism, her work lacked a certain personality and feeling.

"Before the young Americans could leave, however, this artist insisted that they see examples of her earlier work, before her skills had matured enough for a showing in Moscow. She removed from her closet some photographs of her earlier paintings, paintings that were alive with expression, reflecting warmth and vitality.

"She had given those young Americans a message without ever having to say a negative word about artistic freedom under totalitarianism."

≈

"If we're free to dare (and we are), if we're free to give (and we are), then we're free to shape the future and have within our grasp all that we dream the future will be."

≈

"If we look to the answer as to why for so many years we achieved so much, prospered as no other people on earth, it was because here in this land we unleashed the energy and individual genius of man to a greater extent than has ever been done before."

≈

"To those neighbors and allies who share our freedom, we will strengthen our historic ties and assure them of our support and firm commitment. We will match loyalty with loyalty. . . . As for the enemies of freedom, those who are potential adversaries, they will be reminded that peace is the highest aspiration of the American people. We will negotiate for it, sacrifice for it; we will not surrender for it, now or ever."

≈

"Freedom is not something to be secured in any one moment of time. We must struggle to preserve it every day. And freedom is never more than one generation away from extinction."

∾

"Our Founding Fathers fought not only for our political rights, but also to secure the economic freedoms without which these political freedoms are no more than a shadow."

∾

"We Americans make no secret of our belief in freedom. In fact, it's something of a national pastime."

∾

"Freedom is the recognition that no single person, no single authority or government, has a monopoly on the truth, but that every individual life is infinitely precious, that every one of us put in this world has been put there for a reason and has something to offer."

∾

"People have a right, or an obligation, to take freedom from government, and they must continue the struggle to keep it."

∾

"Trust the people. This is the one irrefutable lesson of the entire postwar period, contradicting the notion that rigid government controls are essential to economic development. The societies which achieved the most spectacular broad-based economic progress in the shortest period of time are not the most tightly controlled, not necessarily the biggest in size, or the wealthiest in natural resources. No, what unites them all is their willingness to believe in the magic of the marketplace."

∾

"We must deal with the world as it is and not the way we would like it to be. If we turn a blind eye and a deaf ear when totalitarian regimes brutalize the hopes and dreams of people, we demean the valor of every person who struggles for human dignity and freedom. And we also demean all those who have given that last full measure of devotion."

On Liberals

Reagan's political opponents were certainly not spared his wit. Even though his remarks were often made with a friendly spirit, Reagan always made sure the distinction between his view of America and the liberals'/ Democrats' view was made clear, as the following statements illustrate.

"I feel sorry for some Democratic congressmen. I hear they've been going home after a long day at the office, try to go to sleep, and the first thing you know, they're having nightmares that the money they're spending is their own."

∾

"Democratic candidates used to encourage people to work for their country — you know, 'Ask not what your country can do for you, ask what you can do for your country.'

"Well, a few weeks after that inspirational message, they introduced twenty-nine new spending programs of what the country could do for the people."

⁓

In his remarks to an executive forum on April 6, 1986, Reagan said:

"Well, you know, the Democrats have taken special note of every candle I add to my birthday cake. They keep hoping that I won't be able to blow them all out. Because, you know, your wish comes true then; and they know what I'm wishing for."

⁓

During some remarks in Washington, D.C., on February 11, 1988:

"A friend of mine was asked to a costume ball a short time ago. He slapped some egg on his face and went as a liberal economist."

⁓

At the annual dinner of the Conservative Political Action Conference on January 30, 1986, Reagan said:

"And as for those liberals who are finally catching on to the idea there is a conservative movement, they kind of remind me of a cowboy who was out hiking in the desert one day and came across the Grand Canyon. And he said, 'Wow, something sure happened here!'"

⁓

At a Republican National Committee speech on August 17, 1992:

"I used to say to some of those Democrats who chair every committee in the House: 'You need to balance the government's checkbook the same way you balance your own.' Then I learned how they ran the House bank, and I realized that's exactly what they had been doing!"

～

In a Republican National Committee speech on August 17, 1992:

"A lot of liberal Democrats are saying it's time for a change. . . . What we should change is a Democratic Congress. . . . We have a simple slogan for November 1992: clean house!"

～

In a Republican National Committee speech on August 17, 1992:

"They put on quite a production in New York a few weeks ago. You might even call it slick. A stone's throw from Broadway it was, and how appropriate. Over and over they told us they are not the party they were. They kept telling us with straight faces that they're for family values, they're for a strong America, they're for less-intrusive government. And they call me an actor."

～

"I was born in 1911. Indeed, according to the experts, I have exceeded my life expectancy by quite a few years. Now this is a source of great annoyance to some, especially those in the Democratic Party."

～

"The Democrats may remember their lines, but how quickly they forget the lessons of the past. I have witnessed five major wars in my lifetime, and I know how swiftly storm clouds can gather on a peaceful horizon. The next time a Saddam Hussein takes over Kuwait, or North Korea brandishes a nuclear weapon, will we be ready to respond? In the end, it all comes down to leadership, and that is what this country is looking for now."

≈

This is attributed to Ronald Reagan, and certainly shows the stamp of his wit and humor:

"Republicans believe every day is the Fourth of July, but Democrats believe every day is April fifteenth."

≈

At the Republican National Committee's 1994 gala on the occasion of his eighty-third birthday in Washington, D.C., on February 3, 1994, Reagan said:

"Our friends in the other party will never forgive us for our success and are doing everything in their power to rewrite history. Listening to the liberals, you'd think that the 1980s were the worst period since the Great Depression — filled with greed and despair. Well, you and I know better than that."

≈

"Well, the trouble with our liberal friends is not that they are ignorant, but that they know so much that isn't so!"

~

"Most South Carolinians are, as I am, relatively new converts to Republicanism. We all started out as Democrats, but somehow the Democratic Party went away and left us."

~

"Back in 1980, when the American people saw that they'd gotten talk, not results, who did they call? Well, they called me and George, the malaise-busters."

~

"You know, there are only two things that the liberals don't understand: the things that change and the things that don't. The economy and technology — these things change, and under us they change for the better. But America's basic moral, spiritual, and family values — they don't change."

~

In his remarks at the welcoming rally at the Republican National Convention in New Orleans, Louisiana, on August 14, 1988, Reagan said:

"And you know, we didn't just see at that [Democratic] convention the desire to forget about the record of chaos [Democrats'] policies gave America in the seventies. We also heard them openly saying they're going to steal our words and slogans — words like 'communication,' 'family,' 'values.' And even more amazing, after eight years of prophesying gloom and predicting doom every night on the evening news, they now want to be — and are you ready for this — 'optimistic and hopeful.'"

~

Remarks at the welcoming rally at the Republican National Convention in New Orleans, Louisiana, on August 14, 1988:

"We Republicans love our bandwagon, but all that other party's got is 'a streetcar named desire.'"

~

Reagan once commented on the changes he had seen in the Democratic Party from the time he voted for F.D.R. to the present, and on why he had become a Republican in between:

"What the Democrats had done to this country reminds me of the little girl who said to her mother, 'You know that beautiful jug you told me had been handed down in our family from generation to generation?' And her mother said, 'Yes, what about it?' She said, 'Well, this generation just dropped it.'"

THE FINAL CHAPTER

Coping with Illness

Reagan's humor saw him through some especially critical times with his health. A September 10, 1989, *Los Angeles Times* article reported that after a surgical procedure that drained excess blood from the surface of his brain, Reagan was in good spirits. Afterward he joked about a portion of his head that had to be shaved for the procedure:

"I guess my barber can have the week off."

∾

According to a story the Associated Press ran on March 21, 1989, regarding a forty-minute videotape called "Stand-up Reagan," Reagan said in one excerpt:

"When I go in for a physical, they no longer ask how old I am. They just carbon date me."

∾

The *Indianapolis News* reported on November 10, 1994, that Reagan had been diagnosed with Alzheimer's disease. In a letter making his condition public, he displayed characteristic optimism:

"At the moment I feel just fine. I intend to live the remainder of the years God gives me on this earth doing the things I have always done. I will continue to share life's journey with my beloved Nancy and my family. I plan to enjoy the great outdoors and stay in touch with my friends and supporters."

∾

He also wrote:

"Unfortunately, as Alzheimer's disease progresses, the family often bears a heavy burden. I only wish there was some way I could spare Nancy from this painful experience. When the time comes I am confident that with your help she will face it with faith and courage. . . . In closing let me thank you, the American people, for giving me the great honor of allowing me to serve as your President. When the Lord calls me home, whenever that may be, I will leave with the greatest love for this country of ours and eternal optimism for its future. . . . I now begin the journey that will lead me into the sunset of my life. I know that for America there will always be a bright dawn ahead."

Nancy

When Ronald Reagan met Nancy Davis, he met a rare woman who was not only special enough to be the love of his life, but a woman who was also up to the task of being the First Lady of California and then the United States. The Reagans were openly affectionate with each other in public, and Reagan often paid tribute to his wife.

In the acknowledgments of his book *An American Life*, Reagan wrote:

"First of all, I thank my beloved wife, Nancy. There are really no words to describe what she means to me. Life with her is everything I always hoped it would be."

~

He said Nancy always had an extra instinct to protect:

"She's a nest builder and defender of her own. If you've seen a picture of a bear rearing up on its hind legs when its mate or one of its cubs is in danger, you have a pretty good idea of how Nancy responds to someone who she thinks is trying to hurt or betray one of hers."

~

"If ever God gave me evidence that He had a plan for me, it was the night He brought Nancy into my life."

~

Like any couple, the Reagans had a few differences from each other. Reagan said he had a philosophy class in college in which his professor told the class that the world was divided into two kinds of people: those who are skeptical of others until other persons prove themselves, and those who assume that other people are good and decent unless proven otherwise:

"Maybe [this] describes a difference between Nancy and me. I believe, in general, people are inherently good and expect the best of them. Nancy sees the goodness in people but also has an extra instinct that allows her to see flaws if any are there."

~

It seems that only when it came to Nancy Reagan could her husband be rendered speechless:

"I have spent many hours of my life giving speeches and expressing my opinions. But it is almost impossible for me to express fully how deeply I love Nancy and how much she has filled my life."

~

"Sometimes, I think my life really began when I met Nancy."

~

When asked what quality he most admired in his wife, Reagan replied:

"I can only tell you that knowing her and being married to her is kind of like coming into a warm fire-lit room when you've been out in the cold. I admire her strength and ability. She is a tiny little thing, but I once nicknamed her a peewee powerhouse. . . . She believes in the family, and she was a very successful actress — young actress when we were married. But after we were married, on a lesson from her mother, she said to me, "Well, now, this is my career, and I'm not going to have that career because maybe some people can do both, but I can't.""

~

Reagan was also grateful for his wife's generosity when he recalled his wedding proposal:

"Pretty soon, Nancy was the only one I was calling for dates. And one night over dinner as we sat at a table for two, I said, 'Let's get married.'

"She deserved a more romantic proposal than that, but — bless her — she put her hand on mine, looked into my eyes, and said, 'Let's.'"

~

When reflecting on their first years together, Reagan said:

"From the start, our marriage was like an adolescent's dream of what marriage should be. It was rich and full from the beginning, and it has gotten more so with each passing day."

~

Reagan said his wife's way of dealing with attacks on him was to "get into a hot bath and hold an imaginary conversation with [whoever had taken after him]." Reagan also said:

"I wish I had been able to find as easy a way to deal with attacks on her. In some ways Nancy and I are like one human being: When one of us has a problem, it automatically becomes a problem for the other; an attack on one of us is an attack on both of us. When one suffers, so does the other."

~

"Over the years, I've often felt guilty that so much flack meant for me was aimed at Nancy. When somebody would say something untruthful or nasty about Nancy and I'd get upset about it, people would say, 'Oh, that's just politics.' Well, I never agreed with that or got used to it. There is no justification for a political opponent or someone in the press to go after a man's wife just because he's in politics."

~

In an interview, Reagan told this story to illustrate what lengths his wife would go to for her children:

The Final Chapter

"When our son Ron was fifteen, he dared us to go backpacking with him because he wanted proof that we still loved the outdoor life after the time we spent in Sacramento. Nancy and I discussed it and we proposed a four-day pack trip on horseback into the High Sierra. Ron accepted enthusiastically and it became a first for all of us. We spent long hours in the saddle, and our evenings around a campfire; we slept in sleeping bags, and caught trout for breakfast.

"On the final afternoon we took a narrow switchback trail down into the Yosemite Valley — a trail that had been cut into the side of a sheer, three-thousand-foot cliff. It was only when we were in the valley that I called Nancy's attention to the route we took and for the first time she realized where she had been. Nancy had a fear of heights, but she never allowed that to get in the way of our family activity. Ron told her during the trip, 'Mom, you're doing all right. I really thought you'd last about one day and then find an excuse to go home.'

"Nancy said later that General Custer and the Seventh Cavalry couldn't have driven her out of those mountains after she heard that praise from her son."

∿

And of course it was Nancy who made the White House feel like home for the President:

"During the eight years we lived in the White House, it became a real *home* because Nancy worked to make it that way. I never stopped missing California; I've often said that a Californian (even one transplanted from the Midwest like me) who has to live someplace else lives in a perpetual state of homesickness. California, I like to say, isn't a place, it's a way of life. I once told Margaret Thatcher that her people should have crossed the other ocean to get to this continent; that way the capital of the United States would have been in California. But Nancy made the White House into a wonderful home for us, furnishing it with our things from home, and I felt very comfortable there — it was home.

~

President Reagan took great pride in his wife's involvement in the fight against drug abuse in this country:

"As First Lady, Nancy took it upon herself to turn our fight against drug abuse into a national crusade. She started long before it became a popular political issue, and I think Nancy deserves a tremendous amount of credit for mobilizing the American people against drugs. One young person asked Nancy's advice about what to do when someone offers you drugs. And her answer was so simple and eloquent. She said, 'Just say no.' Today, there are twelve thousand Just Say No clubs around the country encouraging youngsters to spare themselves and their families the pain, the suffering, and, yes, even the death that can come from drug abuse. I am very proud of her."

~

Reagan also admired the First Lady's response when photographers were using powerful lenses to invade their privacy: "Nancy got back at them, though. When she knew the cameras were looking down on us, she waved a sign with just three little words on it, the slogan of her antidrug campaign: JUST SAY NO."

"I can sum up our marriage in a line I spoke when I played the great pitcher Grover Cleveland Alexander, a line spoken by him to his wife, Aimee: 'God must think a lot of me to have given me you.'"

Philosophy of Life

One thing can be said of Reagan that cannot often be said of politicians: he had a constant philosophy of life, not one that flip-flopped with changing political fashions. This philosophy was first impressed upon him by his parents, and it stayed with him throughout his acting and political careers.

He often reflected on his mother's rationale:

"My mother — a small woman with auburn hair and a sense of optimism that ran as deep as the cosmos — told me that everything in life happened for a purpose. She said all things were a part of God's plan, even the most disheartening setbacks, and in the end, everything worked out for the best. . . . My mother, as usual, was right."

~

The importance of hard work and every individual's capacity for it was a keystone in Reagan's philosophy:

"[My father] passed on to me . . . the belief that all men and women, regardless of their color or religion, are created equal and that individuals determine their own destiny; that is, it's largely their own ambition and hard work that determine their fate in life."

~

When a horse belonging to Reagan's daughter, Patty Davis, died — practically her favorite thing in the world — she cried. But her father did not cry. She asked why, and Reagan told her: "Because I'm thinking of all the good times we had together, all the memories I'll have of her. Even though she's gone, I'll always have those."

∽

In calling the Soviet Union the "evil empire" and describing it, as he said, "as it actually was," Reagan felt his sheer honesty about communism was nothing but necessary:

"I've always believed . . . that it's important to define differences, because there are decisions and choices to be made in life and history."

∽

Reagan told *Fortune* magazine on September 15, 1986, his philosophy of leadership:

"Surround yourself with the best people you can find, delegate authority, and don't interfere."

∽

"But someplace along the line to each of us, I suppose, must come that first moment of accepting responsibility. If we don't accept it (and some don't), then we must just grow older without quite growing up."

∽

Remarks by Reagan at the Republican National Committee's 1994 gala on the occasion of his eighty-third birthday in Washington, D.C., on February 3, 1994:

"Now, as most of you know, I'm not one for looking back. I figure there will be plenty of time for that when I get old. But rather what I take from the past is inspiration for the future."

~

"The cynics may call it corny, but this way of life we all cherish is best summed up in three simple words: The American Dream."

~

Reagan, in speaking to a gathering of his federal appointees, said:

"As the old saying goes, 'When you're up to your armpits in alligators, it's sometimes hard to remember that your original intention was to drain the swamp.'"

~

"I'm an optimist. If I wasn't, I would have never left the ranch to come here in the first place. There is a simple definition for an optimist and a pessimist. An optimist asks, 'Will you please pass the cream?' A pessimist says, 'Is there any milk in that pitcher?'"

God and Religion

Throughout his life, Reagan had faith in God. He never tried outright to convert people as he spoke of his faith. He truly believed that "Every single

American is free to choose and practice his or her religious beliefs or to choose no religion at all." It was more that he wanted to share something that had been important to him in his life.

Demonstrating that he is at ease talking about religion, Reagan told this story before a group at the National Association of Manufacturers in 1985:

"It has to do with an old farmer that took over some creek land down there in a creek bottom, never had been farmed before, covered with rocks and brush. And he worked and he cleared away the brush and he had the rocks hauled away and he fertilized and he cultivated and he planted. And he really created a garden spot. And he was so proud of that that one day at church he asked the preacher if he wouldn't come out and see what he'd accomplished. Well, the preacher went out there and he took one look. And he said: 'I've never seen anything like it. These melons, these are the biggest melons I've ever seen. The Lord certainly blessed this land.' And he went on, the tallest corn that he'd ever seen and the squash and the tomatoes and the string beans, everything. And every time he was praising the Lord for all of this. And the old boy was getting pretty fidgety. And finally he couldn't stand it anymore and he said, 'Reverend, I wish you could have seen this when the Lord was doing it by himself.'"

~

To the Conservative Political Action Conference on March 20, 1981, he said:

"When our struggle seems hard, remember what Eric Liddell, Scotland's Olympic champion runner, said in *Chariots of Fire*. He said, 'So where does the power come from to see the race to its end? From within. God made me for a purpose, and I will run for His pleasure.' If we trust in Him, keep His word, and live our lives for His pleasure, He'll give us the power we need — power to fight the good fight, to finish the race, and to keep the faith."

∾

To the National Religious Broadcasters on January 30, 1984:

"If the Lord is our light, our strength, and our salvation, whom shall we fear? Of whom shall we be afraid? No matter where we live, we have a promise that can make all the difference, a promise from Jesus to soothe our sorrows, heal our hearts, and drive away our fears. He promised there will never be a dark night that does not end. Our weeping may endure for a night, but joy cometh in the morning. He promised if our hearts are true, His love will be as sure as sunlight. And, by dying for us, Jesus showed how far our love should be ready to go: all the way."

∾

When Patty was a little girl, somebody told her that whenever there's a shooting star, an angel dies. To comfort Patty, her father told her, "Angels don't die. They'll always be there to keep God company."

∾

He also told Patty when she was a little girl, "God always listens, and He's always watching."

∾

During the 1984 presidential campaign, religion was often foremost on Reagan's mind. Here is what he said in Salt Lake City on September 4, 1984:

"Morality derives chiefly from religious faith. Religion is one of the traditional values which deserves to be preserved and strengthened."

∾

In August 1984, during the campaign for reelection, he said:

"The truth is, politics and morality are inseparable, and as morality's foundation is religion, religion and politics are necessarily related. We need religion as a guide."

A Final Word

Perhaps the most remarkable thing about Ronald Reagan is that he had a soul large enough to recognize that differences in people should be celebrated, and that what has made the United States the most wonderful country in the world is that it is a large enough place, geographically and spiritually, to be home to all the different people who came to live here. He dedicated much of his life to ensuring that America would always be a place where the American Dream is possible.

"The dreams of people may differ, but everyone wants their dreams to come true. Not everybody aspires to be a bank president or a nuclear scientist, but everybody wants to do something with one's life that will give him or her pride and a sense of accomplishment. And America, above all places, gives us the freedom to do that, the freedom to reach out and make our dreams come true."